Hänsel und Gretel und andere Kindermärchen

Hansel and Gretel and other Grimm Fairy Tales

[Bilingual Edition]

German – English

by Jacob and Wilhelm Grimm

Translated by Möwenstein

ISBN: 979-8-89513-204-3

Original text: *Hansel and Gretel and other Grimm Fairy Tales* (1812) by Jacob Grimm (1785-1863) and Wilhelm Grimm (1786-1859)

This bilingual edition—including translation, editorial revisions, formatting, and supplementary content—is produced and edited by Mowenstein Books LLC, with the original text faithfully reproduced from public-domain sources.

While every effort has been made to ensure accuracy, minor discrepancies may occur. Readers are encouraged to consult the original text for reference.

Cover Art: Inspired by *Hustling Sunlight* by Matthew Bakkom (www.hustlingsunlight.xyz)

Möwenstein Books™ is a trademark of and imprint published by Mowenstein Books LLC.

For permissions or inquiries:
Website: mowenstein.com
Email: copyright@mowenstein.com

Mowenstein Books LLC
DE, USA

Contents

Katze und Maus in Gesellschaft

Cat and Mouse in Company

1.1 Eine Katze hatte Bekanntschaft mit einer Maus gemacht und ihr soviel von der großen Liebe und Freundschaft vorgesagt, die sie zu ihr trüge, daß die Maus endlich einwilligte, mit ihr zusammen in einem Hause zu wohnen und gemeinschaftliche Wirtschaft zu führen.

A cat had made the acquaintance of a mouse and told her so much about the great love and friendship she had for her that the mouse finally agreed to live with her in a house and keep house together.

1.2 »Aber für den Winter müssen wir Vorsorge tragen,

"But we must take precautions for the winter,

1.3 sonst leiden wir Hunger.« sagte die Katze,

otherwise we shall go hungry." said the cat,

1.4 »du, Mäuschen, kannst dich nicht überall hinwagen und gerätst mir am Ende in eine Falle.«

"you, little mouse, cannot venture everywhere and will end up in a trap."

1

Der gute Rat ward also befolgt und ein Töpfchen mit Fett angekauft. 1.5

So the good advice was followed and a pot of fat was bought.

Sie wußten aber nicht wo sie es hinstellen sollten, endlich nach langer Überlegung sprach die Katze: 1.6

But they didn't know where to put it, and finally, after much deliberation, the cat said:

»Ich weiß keinen Ort, wo es besser aufgehoben wäre, als die Kirche, da getraut sich niemand etwas wegzunehmen; 1.7

"I don't know of anywhere better to put it than the church, where nobody dares to take anything away;

wir stellen es unter den Altar und rühren es nicht eher an als bis wir es nötig haben.« 1.8

we'll put it under the altar and not touch it until we need it."

Das Töpfchen ward also in Sicherheit gebracht, aber es dauerte nicht lange, so trug die Katze Gelüsten danach und sprach zur Maus: 1.9

So the potty was put in a safe place, but it was not long before the cat had a craving for it and said to the mouse:

»Was ich dir sagen wollte, Mäuschen, ich bin von meiner Base zu Gevatter gebeten: 1.10

"What I wanted to tell you, little mouse, I have been asked by my base to be a godfather:

sie hat ein Söhnchen zur Welt gebracht, weiß mit braunen Flecken, das soll ich über die Taufe halten. 1.11

she has given birth to a little son, white with brown spots, which I am to hold over the baptism.

1.12 Laß mich heute ausgehen und besorge du das Haus allein.«

Let me go out to-day, and you take care of the house alone. "

1.13 »Ja, ja.« antwortete die Maus,

"Yes, yes." replied the mouse,

1.14 »geh in Gottes Namen, wenn du was Gutes ißest, so denk an mich;

"go in God's name, when you eat something good, think of me;

1.15 von dem süßen roten Kindbetterwein tränk ich auch gerne ein Tröpfchen.«

I will gladly drink a drop of the sweet red baby wine. "

1.16 Es war aber alles nicht wahr,

But none of this was true,

1.17 die Katze hatte keine Base und war nicht zu Gevatter gebeten.

the cat had no base and had not been asked to be a godmother.

1.18 Sie ging geradeswegs nach der Kirche, schlich zu dem Fetttöpfchen, fing an zu lecken und leckte die fette Haut ab.

She went straight to the church, crept to the fat pot, began to lick and licked the fat skin.

1.19 Dann machte sie einen Spaziergang auf den Dächern der Stadt, besah sich die Gelegenheit, streckte sich hernach in der Sonne aus und wischte sich den Bart, so oft sie an das Fetttöpfchen dachte.

Then she took a walk on the roofs of the town, looked at the opportunity, then stretched out in the sun and wiped her beard as often as she thought of the fat pot.

Erst als es Abend war, kam sie wieder nach Haus. »Nun,

1.20

It wasn't until evening that she returned home. "Well,

da bist du ja wieder.« sagte die Maus,

1.21

there you are again." said the mouse,

»du hast gewiß einen lustigen Tag gehabt.«

1.22

"you must have had a fun day."

»Es ging wohl an.« antwortete die Katze.

1.23

"I guess it started." replied the cat.

»Was hat denn das Kind für einen Namen bekommen?«

1.24

"What kind of name did the child get?"

fragte die Maus. »Hautab.« sagte die Katze ganz trocken.

1.25

asked the mouse. "Hautab ." said the cat dryly.

»Hautab.« rief die Maus,

1.26

"Hautab." exclaimed the mouse,

»das ist ja ein wunderlicher und seltsamer Name,

1.27

"that's a strange and peculiar name,

ist der in eurer Familie gebräuchlich?«

1.28

is it common in your family?"

»Was ist da weiter.« sagte die Katze,

1.29

"What's more." said the cat,

»er ist nicht schlechter als Bröseldieb,

1.30

"it's no worse than crumb thief,

1.31 wie deine Paten heißen.«

as your godparents are called."

2.1 Nicht lange danach überkam die Katze wieder ein Gelüsten.

Not long afterwards the cat was again overcome by a craving.

2.2 Sie sprach zur Maus:

She said to the mouse,

2.3 »Du mußt mir den Gefallen thun und nochmals das Hauswesen allein besorgen, ich bin zum zweitenmal zu Gevatter gebeten, und da das Kind einen weißen Ring um den Hals hat, so kann ich's nicht absagen.«

"You must do me the favor of doing the housework alone again, I have been asked to be godfather for the second time, and since the child has a white ring around its neck, I cannot refuse."

2.4 Die gute Maus willigte ein,

The good mouse agreed,

2.5 die Katze aber schlich hinter der Stadtmauer zu der Kirche und fraß den Fetttopf halb aus.

but the cat crept behind the city wall to the church and ate half of the pot of fat.

2.6 »Es schmeckt nichts besser.« sagte sie,

"Nothing tastes better." she said,

2.7 »als was man selber ißt.«

"than what you eat yourself."

2.8 und war mit ihrem Tagewerk ganz zufrieden. Als sie heimkam,

and was quite satisfied with her day's work. When she got home,

fragte die Maus: »Wie ist denn dieses Kind getauft worden?«   2.9

the mouse asked: "How was this child baptized?"

»Halbaus« antwortete die Katze. »Halbaus! was du sagst!   2.10

"Halbaus" replied the cat. "Halbaus! what you say!

den Namen habe ich mein Lebtag noch nicht gehört, ich wette, der steht nicht in dem Kalender.«   2.11

I've never heard that name in my life, I bet it's not on the calendar."

Der Katze wässerte das Maul bald wieder nach dem Leckerwerk.   3.1

The cat's mouth was soon watering for the treat again.

»Aller guten Dinge sind drei.« sprach sie zu der Maus.   3.2

"All good things come in threes." she said to the mouse.

»da soll ich wieder Gevatter stehen, das Kind ist ganz schwarz und hat bloß weiße Pfoten, sonst kein weißes Haar am ganzen Leib, das trifft sich alle paar Jahr nur einmal;   3.3

"I'm to be godfather again, the child is all black and has only white paws, otherwise no white hair on the whole body, that only happens once every few years;

du läßt mich doch ausgehen?«   3.4

you'll let me go out, won't you?"

»Hautab! Halbaus!« antwortete die Maus,   3.5

"Skin off! Halbaus!" replied the mouse,

3.6 »es sind so kuriose Namen, die machen mich so nachdenksam.«

"they are such curious names, they make me so thoughtful."

3.7 »Da sitzest du daheim in deinem dunkelgrauen Flausrock und deinem langen Haarzopf.«

"There you sit at home in your dark gray fluffy skirt and your long plait of hair."

3.8 sprach die Katze, »und fängst Grillen;

said the cat, "and catch crickets;

3.9 das kommt davon, wenn man bei Tage nicht ausgeht.«

that's what comes of not going out in the daytime."

3.10 Die Maus räumte während der Abwesenheit der Katze auf und brachte das Haus in Ordnung,

The mouse tidied up during the cat's absence and put the house in order,

3.11 die naschhafte Katze aber fraß den Fetttopf rein aus.

but the sweet-toothed cat ate the fat pot clean.

3.12 »Wenn erst alles aufgezehrt ist, so hat man Ruhe.«

"Once everything has been eaten, you can rest."

3.13 sagte sie zu sich selbst und kam satt und dick erst in der Nacht nach Haus.

she said to herself and came home at night, full and fat.

3.14 Die Maus fragte gleich nach dem Namen, den das dritte Kind bekommen hätte.

The mouse immediately asked what name the third child had been given.

»Er wird dir wohl auch nicht gefallen.« sagte die
Katze,

3.15

"You probably won't like it either." said the cat,

»er heißt Ganzaus.«

3.16

"it's called Ganzaus ."

»Ganzaus!« rief die Maus,

3.17

"Ganzaus!" cried the mouse,

»gedruckt ist er mir noch nicht vorgekommen.
Ganzaus!

3.18

"I've never seen him in print before. Ganzaus!

was soll das bedeuten?« Sie schüttelte den Kopf,

3.19

What does that mean?" She shook her head,

rollte sich zusammen und legte sich schlafen.

3.20

curled up and went to sleep.

Von nun an wollte niemand mehr die Katze zu
Gevatter bitten;

4.1

From then on, no one wanted to ask the cat to be their
godfather;

als aber der Winter herangekommen und draußen
nichts mehr zu finden war, gedachte die Maus ihres
Vorrats und sprach:

4.2

but when winter came and there was nothing left outside,
the mouse thought of her supplies and said,

»Komm Katze, wir wollen zu unserem Fetttopfe
gehen, den wir uns aufgespart haben, der wird uns
schmecken.«

4.3

"Come on, cat, let's go to the fat pot we've been saving,
we'll like it."

4.4 »Ja, wohl.« antwortete die Katze,
"Yes, well." replied the cat,

4.5 »der wird dir schmecken, als wenn du deine feine Zunge zum Fenster hinausstreckst.«
"it will taste better to you than sticking your fine tongue out of the window."

4.6 Sie machten sich auf den Weg, und als sie anlangten, stand zwar der Fetttopf noch an seinem Platz, er war aber leer.
They set off, and when they arrived, the pot of fat was still in its place, but it was empty.

4.7 »Ach.« sagte die Maus,
"Oh." said the mouse,

4.8 »jetzt merke ich was geschehen ist, jetzt kommt's an den Tag, du bist mir die wahre Freundin!
"now I realize what has happened, now it's coming to light, you are my true friend!

4.9 Aufgefressen hast du alles, wie du zu Gevatter gestanden hast:
You've eaten everything, just like you stood by my father:

4.10 erst Haut ab, dann halb aus, dann ...«
first skin off, then half off, then ..."

4.11 »Willst du schweigen.« rief die Katze,
"Will you be silent." cried the cat,

4.12 »noch ein Wort, und ich fresse dich auf.«
"one more word and I'll eat you up."

4.13 »Ganz aus.«
"All out."

hatte die arme Maus schon auf der Zunge, kaum 4.14
war es heraus, so that die Katze einen Satz nach ihr,
packte sie und schluckte sie hinunter.
The poor mouse already had it on the tip of her tongue, but
as soon as it was out, the cat made a dash for it, grabbed it
and swallowed it down.

Siehst du, so geht's in der Welt. 4.15
You see, that's the way of the world.

Der gute Handel

The Good Trade

1.1 Ein Bauer, der hatte seine Kuh auf den Markt getrieben und für sieben Thaler verkauft.
A farmer had driven his cow to market and sold it for seven thalers.

1.2 Auf dem Heimwege mußte er an einem Teich vorbei,
On his way home he had to pass a pond,

1.3 und da hörte er schon von weitem wie die Frösche riefen:
and there he heard the frogs calling from afar:

1.4 »Ak, ak, ak, ak.«
"Ak, ak, ak, ak."

1.5 »Ja.« sprach er für sich,
"Yes." he said to himself,

1.6 »die schreien auch ins Haberfeld hinein;
"they are screaming into the Haberfeld too;

1.7 sieben sind's, die ich gelöst habe, keine acht.«
there are seven of them that I have solved, not eight."

Als er zu dem Wasser herankam, rief er ihnen zu:

1.8

As he approached the water, he called out to them:

»Dummes Vieh, das ihr seid! wißt ihr's nicht besser?

1.9

"Stupid cattle that you are! Don't you know any better?

sieben Thaler sind's und keine acht.«

1.10

There are seven thalers and not eight."

Die Frösche blieben aber bei ihrem »ak, ak, ak, ak.«

1.11

But the frogs stuck to their "ak, ak, ak, ak, ak."

»Nun, wenn ihr's nicht glauben wollt, ich kann's euch vorzählen.«

1.12

"Well, if you don't want to believe it, I can count it for you."

holte das Geld aus der Tasche und zählte die sieben Thaler ab,

1.13

He took the money out of his pocket and counted out the seven thalers,

immer vierundzwanzig Groschen auf einen.

1.14

always twenty-four pennies to one.

Die Frösche kehrten sich aber nicht an seine Rechnung und riefen abermals:

1.15

The frogs, however, did not pay any attention to his count and called out again:

»Ak, ak, ak, ak.«

1.16

"Ak, ak, ak, ak."

»Ei.« rief der Bauer ganz bös,

1.17

"Egg." shouted the farmer quite crossly,

1.18 »wollt ihr's besser wissen als ich, so zählt selber.«

"if you want to know better than I do, count for yourselves."

1.19 und warf ihnen das Geld miteinander ins Wasser hinein.

and threw the money into the water with them.

1.20 Er blieb stehen und wollte warten, bis sie fertig wären und ihm das Seinige wiederbrächten, aber die Frösche beharrten auf ihrem Sinn, schrien immerfort:

He stood still and wanted to wait until they had finished and brought him back what was his, but the frogs insisted and kept shouting:

1.21 »Ak, ak, ak, ak.«

"Ak, ak, ak, ak, ak."

1.22 und warfen auch das Geld nicht wieder heraus.

and did not throw the money out again.

1.23 Er wartete noch eine gute Weile, bis der Abend anbrach, und er nach Hause mußte, da schimpfte er die Frösche aus und rief:

He waited a good while longer, till evening came on, and he had to go home, when he scolded the frogs, and cried,

1.24 »Ihr Wasserpatscher, ihr Dickköpfe, ihr Klotzaugen, ein groß Maul habt ihr und könnt schreien, daß einem die Ohren wehthun, aber sieben Thaler könnt ihr nicht zählen:

"You water-patchers, you thick-heads, you block-eyes, you have big mouths, and you can shout so that your ears hurt, but you can't count seven thalers:

meint ihr, ich wollte da stehen, bis ihr fertig wärt?«   1.25

do you think I would stand there till you had finished?"

Damit ging er fort, aber die Frösche riefen noch   1.26

With that he went away, but the frogs were still shouting

»ak, ak, ak, ak« hinter ihm her,   1.27

"ak, ak, ak, ak, ak" after him,

daß er ganz verdrießlich heimkam.   1.28

so that he came home quite annoyed.

Über eine Zeit erhandelte er sich wieder eine Kuh,   2.1
die schlachtete er, und machte die Rechnung, wenn
er das Fleisch gut verkaufte, könnte er soviel lösen,
als die beiden Kühe wert wären, und das Fell hätte er
obendrein.

After a time he bought another cow, which he slaughtered,
and calculated that if he sold the meat well, he could get as
much as the two cows were worth, and he would have the
hide to boot.

Als er nun mit dem Fleisch zu der Stadt kam,   2.2
war vor dem Thore ein ganzes Rudel Hunde
zusammengelaufen, voran ein großer Windhund:
der sprang um das Fleisch, schnupperte und bellte,

When he came to the town with the meat, a whole pack
of dogs had gathered outside the gate, led by a large
greyhound, who jumped around the meat, sniffed and
barked,

»Was, was, was, was.« Als er gar nicht aufhören   2.3
wollte,

"What, what, what, what." When he wouldn't stop,

14

2.4 **sprach der Bauer zu ihm: »Ja, ich merke wohl, du sagst**
the farmer said to him: "Yes, I see you're saying

2.5 **»was, was.«**
"what, what, what."

2.6 **weil du etwas von dem Fleisch verlangst, da sollt ich aber schön ankommen, wenn ich dir's geben wollte.«**
because you want some of the meat, but I'd better get there if I wanted to give it to you."

2.7 **Der Hund antwortete nichts als »was, was.«**
The dog replied nothing but "what, what."

2.8 **»Willst du's auch nicht wegfressen und für deine Kameraden da gut stehen?«**
"Don't you want to eat it away and be good for your companions?"

2.9 **»Was, was.« sprach der Hund.**
"What, what." said the dog.

2.10 **»Nun, wenn du dabei beharrst, so will ich dir's lassen, ich kenne dich wohl und weiß, bei wem du dienst; aber das sage ich dir, in drei Tagen muß ich mein Geld haben, sonst geht dir's schlimm: du kannst mir's nur herausbringen.«**
"Well, if you persist, I will let you have it, I know you well, and with whom you serve; but I tell you this, I must have my money in three days, or you will be in a bad way; you can only bring it out to me."

2.11 **Darauf lud er das Fleisch ab und kehrte wieder um: die Hunde machten sich darüber her und bellten laut,**
Thereupon he unloaded the meat and turned back: the dogs made a rush at it and barked loudly,

»Was, was.«   _{2.12}
"What, what."

Der Bauer, der es von weitem hörte, sprach zu sich: 2.13
The farmer, hearing it from afar, said to himself,

»Horch, jetzt verlangen sie alle was, aber der große   2.14
muß mir einstehen.«
"Listen, now they're all asking for something, but the big
one has to stand up for me."

Als drei Tage herum waren, dachte der Bauer: 3.1
When three days had passed, the farmer thought:

»Heute abend hast du dein Geld in der Tasche«   3.2
"Tonight you'll have your money in your pocket"

und war ganz vergnügt.   3.3
and was quite happy.

Aber es wollte niemand kommen und auszahlen.   3.4
But no one wanted to come and pay out.

»Es ist kein Verlaß mehr auf jemand.«   3.5
"You can't rely on anyone any more."

sprach er, und endlich riß ihm die Geduld, daß er   3.6
in die Stadt zu dem Fleischer ging und sein Geld
forderte.
he said, and finally his patience ran out, so he went into
town to the butcher and demanded his money.

Der Fleischer meinte, es wäre ein Spaß, aber der   3.7
Bauer sagte,
The butcher thought it was a joke, but the farmer said,

3.8 »Spaß beiseite, ich will mein Geld;
"Joking aside, I want my money;

3.9 hat der große Hund euch nicht die ganze geschlachtete Kuh vor drei Tagen heimgebracht?«
didn't the big dog bring you home the whole slaughtered cow three days ago?"

3.10 Da ward der Fleischer zornig,
Then the butcher got angry,

3.11 griff nach einem Besenstiel und jagte ihn hinaus.
grabbed a broomstick and chased him out.

3.12 »Wart«, sagte der Bauer, »es giebt noch Gerechtigkeit auf der Welt!«
"Wait" said the farmer, "there is still justice in the world!"

3.13 und ging in das Königliche Schloß und bat sich Gehör aus.
and he went into the royal palace and begged to be heard.

3.14 Er ward vor den König geführt, der dasaß mit seiner Tochter und fragte, was ihm für ein Leid widerfahren wäre?
He was brought before the King, who sat there with his daughter and asked what harm had befallen him?

3.15 »Ach.« sagte er,
"Alas." said he,

3.16 »die Frösche und die Hunde haben mir das Meinige genommen,
"the frogs and the dogs have taken what was mine,

und der Metzger hat mich dafür mit dem Stock
bezahlt.« 3.17
and the butcher has paid me for it with a stick."

und erzählte weitläufig, wie es zugegangen war. 3.18
and he went on to relate in detail what had happened.

Darüber fing die Königstochter laut an zu lachen, und
der König sprach zu ihm, 3.19
At this the king's daughter began to laugh aloud, and the
king said to him,

»Recht kann ich dir hier nicht geben, 3.20
"I cannot give you justice here,

aber dafür sollst du meine Tochter zur Frau haben; 3.21
but in return you shall have my daughter to wife;

ihr Lebtag hat sie noch nicht gelacht, als eben über
dich, und ich habe sie dem versprochen, der sie zum
Lachen brächte. 3.22
she has never laughed in her life but at you, and I have
promised her to him who would make her laugh.

Du kannst Gott für dein Glück danken.« 3.23
You can thank God for your good fortune."

»O.« antwortete der Bauer, »ich will sie gar nicht; 3.24
"Oh." replied the farmer, "I don't want her at all;

ich habe daheim nur eine einzige Frau, 3.25
I have only one wife at home,

und die ist mir schon zu viel. Wenn ich nach Hause
komme, 3.26
and she is too much for me. When I come home,

3.27 so ist mir nicht anders als ob in jedem Winkel eine stände.«

I feel as if there were one in every corner."

3.28 Da ward der König zornig und sagte: »Du bist ein Grobian.«

Then the king became angry and said, "You are a ruffian."

3.29 »Ach, Herr König.« antwortete der Bauer,

"Oh, Sir King." replied the farmer,

3.30 »was könnt Ihr von einem Ochsen anderes erwarten als Rindfleisch!«

"what else can you expect from an ox but beef!"

3.31 »Warte.« erwiderte der König,

"Wait." replied the king,

3.32 »du sollst einen anderen Lohn haben.

"you shall have another reward.

3.33 Jetzt pack dich fort, aber in drei Tagen komm wieder, so sollen dir fünfhundert vollgezählt werden.«

Now pack off, but come back in three days and you shall be paid five hundred."

4.1 Wie der Bauer hinaus vor die Thür kam, sprach die Schildwache,

As the farmer came out of the door, the guard said,

4.2 »Du hast die Königstochter zum Lachen gebracht,

"You have made the king's daughter laugh,

4.3 da wirst du was rechtes bekommen haben.«

so you will have gotten something right."

»Ja, das mein ich.« antwortete der Bauer, 4.4
"Yes, that's what I mean." replied the farmer,

»fünfhundert werden mir ausgezahlt.« 4.5
"five hundred will be paid to me."

»Hör.« sprach der Soldat, 4.6
"Listen." said the soldier,

»gieb mir etwas davon! Was willst du mit all dem 4.7
Geld anfangen!«
"give me some of it! What are you going to do with all that
money?"

»Weil du's bist.« sprach der Bauer, 4.8
"Because it is you." said the peasant,

»so sollst du zweihundert haben, melde dich in drei 4.9
Tagen beim König, und laß dir's aufzählen.«
"you shall have two hundred; report to the king in three
days, and have it counted out to you."

Ein Jude, der in der Nähe geständen und das 4.10
Gespräch mit angehört hatte, lief dem Bauer nach,
hielt ihn beim Rock und sprach,
A Jew, who had been standing near by, and had overheard
the conversation, ran after the farmer, held him by the
skirt, and said,

»Gottes Wunder, was seid ihr ein Glückskind! 4.11
"God's wonder, what a lucky child you are!

ich will's euch wechseln, ich will's euch umsetzen in 4.12
Scheidemünz, was wollt ihr mit den harten Thalern?«
I will change it for you, I will turn it over to you in
Scheidemünz, what do you want with the hard thalers?"

4.13 »Mauschel.« sagte der Bauer,

"Mauschel." said the peasant,

4.14 »dreihundert kannst du noch haben, gieb mir's gleich in Münze, heute über drei Tage wirst da dafür beim Könige bezahlt werden.«

"you can still have three hundred, give it to me in coin right away, you'll be paid for it by the king today for three days."

4.15 Der Jude freute sich über das Profitchen und brachte die Summe in schlechten Groschen,

The Jew was glad of the little profit and brought the sum in bad pennies,

4.16 wo drei soviel wert sind als zwei gute.

where three are worth as much as two good ones.

4.17 Nach Verlauf der drei Tage ging der Bauer, dem Befehl des Königs gemäß, vor den König.

After the three days had passed, the peasant went before the king as ordered.

4.18 »Zieht ihm den Rock aus.« sprach dieser,

"Take off his coat." said the king,

4.19 »er soll seine fünfhundert haben.«

"he shall have his five hundred."

4.20 »Ach.« sagte der Bauer,

"Alas." said the peasant,

4.21 »sie gehören nicht mehr mein, zweihundert habe ich an die Schildwache verschenkt, und dreihundert hat mir der Jude eingewechselt, von Rechts wegen gebührt mir gar nichts.«

"they are no longer mine; I have given two hundred to the shield-guard, and the Jew has exchanged three hundred for me; by rights I am entitled to nothing."

Indem kam der Soldat und der Jude herein, 4.22
verlangten das Ihrige, das sie dem Bauer abgewonnen
hätten und erhielten die Schläge richtig zugemessen.
Then the soldier and the Jew came in, demanded their
share, which they had taken from the farmer, and received
the blows correctly measured.

Der Soldat ertrug's geduldig und wußte schon wie's 4.23
schmeckte;
The soldier bore it patiently and already knew how it tasted;

der Jude aber hat jämmerlich: »Au weih geschrien! 4.24
but the Jew cried out piteously, "Oh, dear!

sind das die harten Thaler?« 4.25
Are these the hard thalers?"

Der König mußte über den Bauer lachen, und da aller 4.26
Zorn verschwunden war, sprach er:
The king had to laugh at the peasant, and when all his anger
had disappeared, he said,

»Weil du deinen Lohn schon verloren hast, bevor er 4.27
dir zu Teil ward, so will ich dir einen Ersatz geben:
"Because you have lost your wages before they were given
to you, I will give you a substitute:

geh in meine Schatzkammer und hol dir Geld, so viel 4.28
du willst.«
go into my treasury and get as much money as you want."

Der Bauer ließ sich das nicht zweimal sagen und 4.29
füllte in seine weiten Taschen was nur hinein wollte.
The farmer didn't need to be told twice and filled his wide
pockets with whatever he wanted.

4.30 **Danach ging er ins Wirtshaus und überzählte sein Geld.**

He then went into the inn and counted out his money.

4.31 **Der Jude war ihm nachgeschlichen und hörte, wie er mit sich allein brummte:**

The Jew had followed him and heard him muttering to himself:

4.32 **»Nun hat mich der Spitzbube von König doch hinters Licht geführt!**

"Now that rogue of a king has tricked me!

4.33 **Hätte er mir nicht selbst das Geld geben können, so wüßte ich, was ich hätte, wie kann ich nun wissen, ob das richtig ist, was ich so auf gut Glück eingesteckt habe!«**

If he hadn't been able to give me the money himself, I would have known what I had, so how can I know now whether what I've pocketed on the off chance is right!"

4.34 **»Gott bewahre.« sprach der Jude für sich,**

"God forbid." said the Jew to himself,

4.35 **»der spricht despektierlich von unserem Herrn, ich lauf und geb's an, da krieg ich eine Belohnung, und er wird obendrein noch bestraft.«**

"he speaks disrespectfully of our lord, I'll run and tell him, I'll get a reward, and he'll be punished to boot."

4.36 **Als der König von den Reden des Bauern hörte,**

When the king heard what the farmer had said,

4.37 **geriet er in Zorn und hieß den Juden hingehen und den Sünder herbeiholen.**

he was furious and ordered the Jew to go and fetch the sinner.

Der Jude lief zum Bauer: 4.38
The Jew ran to the farmer:

»Ihr sollt gleich zum Herrn König kommen, wie Ihr   4.39
geht und steht.«
"You should come straight to the king as you go and as you
stand."

»Ich weiß besser, was sich schickt.« antwortete der   4.40
Bauer,
"I know better what to do." answered the peasant,

»erst laß ich mir einen neuen Rock machen;   4.41
"first I will have a new coat made;

meinst du, ein Mann, der soviel Geld in der Tasche   4.42
hat, sollte in dem alten Lumpenrock hingehen?«
do you think a man who has so much money in his pocket
should go in the old rag coat?"

Der Jude, als er sah, daß der Bauer ohne einen   4.43
anderen Rock nicht wegzubringen war, und weil
er fürchtete, wenn der Zorn des Königs verraucht
wäre, so käme er um seine Belohnung und der Bauer
um seine Strafe, so sprach er:
The Jew, when he saw that the peasant could not be taken
away without another coat, and because he feared that if
the king's wrath were spent, he would lose his reward and
the peasant his punishment, said,

»Ich will Euch für die kurze Zeit einen schönen Rock   4.44
leihen aus bloßer Freundschaft;
"I will lend you a nice coat for a short time out of mere
friendship;

was thut der Mensch nicht alles aus Liebe!«   4.45
what does a man not do out of love!"

24

4.46 **Der Bauer ließ sich das gefallen,**
The peasant accepted this,

4.47 **zog den Rock vom Juden an und ging mit ihm fort.**
put on the Jew's coat and went away with him.

4.48 **Der König hielt dem Bauer die bösen Reden vor, die der Jude hinterbracht hatte.**
The king reproached the peasant with the evil words which the Jew had uttered.

4.49 **»Ach.« sprach der Bauer,**
"Ah." said the peasant,

4.50 **»was ein Jude sagt, ist immer gelogen, dem geht kein wahres Wort aus dem Munde;**
"what a Jew says is always a lie, no true word comes out of his mouth;

4.51 **der Kerl da ist imstande und behauptet, ich hätte seinen Rock an.«**
that fellow is able to say that I have his coat on."

4.52 **»Was soll mir das?« schrie der Jude,**
"What is this to me?" cried the Jew,

4.53 **»ist der Rock nicht mein?**
"isn't the skirt mine?

4.54 **Hab ich ihn Euch nicht aus bloßer Freundschaft geborgt, damit Ihr vor den Herrn König treten konntet?«**
Did I not lend it to you out of mere friendship so that you could appear before the king?"

4.55 **Wie der König das hörte, sprach er,**
When the king heard this, he said,

»Einen hat der Jude gewiß betrogen,   4.56

"The Jew has certainly deceived one person,

mich oder den Bauer.«   4.57

either me or the peasant."

und ließ ihm noch etwas in harten Thalern   4.58
nachzahlen.

and made him pay a little more in hard thalers.

Der Bauer aber ging in dem guten Rock und mit dem   4.59
guten Geld in der Tasche heim und sprach,

But the peasant went home in his good coat and with the
good money in his pocket, and said,

»Diesmal hab ich's getroffen.«   4.60

"This time I have done it."

Der wunderliche Spielmann

The Whimsical Minstrel

1.1 Es war einmal ein wunderlicher Spielmann, der ging durch einen Wald mutterseelen allein und dachte hin und her, und als für seine Gedanken nichts mehr übrig war, sprach er zu sich selbst,

Once upon a time there was a wondrous minstrel who walked through a forest alone, thinking to and fro, and when there was nothing left for his thoughts, he said to himself,

1.2 »Mir wird hier im Walde Zeit und Weile lang,

"I'm running out of time here in the forest,

1.3 ich will einen guten Gesellen herbeiholen.«

I want to fetch a good journeyman."

1.4 Da nahm er die Geige vom Rücken und fiedelte eins, daß es durch alle Bäume schallte.

So he took the fiddle from his back and played it so loudly that it rang through all the trees.

1.5 Nicht lange, so kam ein Wolf durch das Dickicht dahergetrabt.

It was not long before a wolf came trotting through the thicket.

27

»Ach, ein Wolf kommt! nach dem trage ich kein
Verlangen.«

1.6

"Oh, a wolf is coming! I have no desire for him."

sagte der Spielmann;

1.7

said the minstrel;

aber der Wolf schritt näher und sprach zu ihm:

1.8

but the wolf came nearer and said to him,

»Ei, du lieber Spielmann, was fiedelst du so schön!

1.9

"Oh, you dear minstrel, what a beautiful fiddle you play!

das möcht ich auch lernen.«

1.10

I would like to learn that too."

»Das ist bald gelernt.« antwortete ihm der
Spielmann,

1.11

"That will soon be learned." answered the minstrel,

»du mußt nur alles thun, was ich dich heiße.«

1.12

"you must only do everything I bid you."

»O Spielmann.« sprach der Wolf,

1.13

"O minstrel." said the wolf,

»ich will dir gehorchen, wie ein Schüler seinem
Meister.«

1.14

"I will obey you as a pupil obeys his master."

Der Spielmann hieß ihn mitgehen, und als sie ein
Stück Weges zusammen gegangen waren, kamen sie
an einen alten Eichbaum, der innen hohl und in der
Mitte aufgerissen war.

1.15

The minstrel bade him go with him, and when they had
gone a little way together, they came to an old oak-tree,
which was hollow inside and torn open in the middle.

1.16 »Sieh her.« sprach der Spielmann,
"Look here." said the minstrel,

1.17 »willst du fiedeln lernen,
"if you want to learn to play the fiddle,

1.18 so lege die Vorderpfoten in diesen Spalt.«
put your front paws in this crack."

1.19 Der Wolf gehorchte, aber der Spielmann hob schnell einen Stein auf und keilte ihm die beiden Pfoten mit einem Schlag so fest, daß er wie ein Gefangener da liegen bleiben mußte.
The wolf obeyed, but the minstrel quickly picked up a stone and with one blow wedged his two paws so firmly that he had to lie there like a prisoner.

1.20 »Warte da solange, bis ich wieder komme.«
"Wait there until I come back."

1.21 sagte der Spielmann und ging seines Weges.
said the minstrel, and went his way.

2.1 Über eine Weile sprach er abermals zu sich selber:
After a while, he said to himself again:

2.2 »Mir wird hier im Walde Zeit und Weile lang,
"I'm running out of time here in the forest,

2.3 ich will einen anderen Gesellen herbeiholen.«
I want to fetch another journeyman."

2.4 nahm seine Geige und fiedelte wieder in den Wald hinein.
He took his violin and fiddled off into the forest again.

Nicht lange, so kam ein Fuchs durch die Bäume dahergeschlichen. 2.5
Before long, a fox came sneaking through the trees.

»Ach, ein Fuchs kommt!« sagte der Spielmann, 2.6
"Oh, a fox is coming!" said the minstrel,

»nach dem trage ich kein Verlangen.« 2.7
"I have no desire for him."

Der Fuchs kam zu ihm heran und sprach: 2.8
The fox came up to him and said,

»Ei, du lieber Spielmann, was fiedelst du so schön! 2.9
"Oh, dear minstrel, what a beautiful fiddle you play!

das möcht ich auch lernen.« 2.10
I'd like to learn that too."

»Das ist bald gelernt.« sprach der Spielmann, 2.11
"That will soon be learned." said the minstrel,

»du mußt nur alles thun, was ich dich heiße.« 2.12
"you must only do everything I bid you."

»O Spielmann.« antwortete der Fuchs, 2.13
"O minstrel." replied the fox,

»ich will dir gehorchen, wie ein Schüler seinem Meister.« 2.14
"I will obey you as a pupil obeys his master."

»Folge mir.« 2.15
"Follow me."

2.16 sagte der Spielmann, und als sie ein Stück Weges gegangen waren, kamen sie auf einen Fußweg, zu dessen beiden Seiten hohe Sträucher standen.

said the minstrel, and when they had gone a little way, they came to a footpath, on either side of which stood tall bushes.

2.17 Da hielt der Spielmann still, bog von der einen Seite ein Haselnußbäumchen zur Erde herab und trat mit dem Fuß auf die Spitze, dann bog er von der andern Seite noch ein Bäumchen herab und sprach:

Then the minstrel stood still, bent down a hazel tree from one side to the ground and stepped on the top of it with his foot, then he bent down another tree from the other side and said,

2.18 »Wohlan, Füchslein, wenn du etwas lernen willst, so reich mir deine linke Vorderpfote.«

"Well, little fox, if you want to learn something, give me your left front paw."

2.19 Der Fuchs gehorchte And der Spielmann band ihm die Pfote an den linken Stamm.

The fox obeyed and the minstrel tied his paw to the left trunk.

2.20 »Füchslein.« sprach er, »nun reich mir die rechte!«

"Little fox." he said, "now hand me your right one!"

2.21 die band er ihm an den rechten Stamm.

He tied it to the right trunk.

Und als er nachgesehen hatte, ob die Knoten der
Stricke auch fest genug waren, ließ er los, und die
Bäumchen fuhren in die Höhe und schnellten das
Füchslein hinauf, daß es in der Luft schwebte und
zappelte.   2.22

And when he had made sure that the knots of the ropes
were tight enough, he let go, and the little trees flew
upwards and whisked the vixen up so that he floated and
wriggled in the air.

»Warte da solange, bis ich wiederkomme.«   2.23

"Wait there till I come back."

sagte der Spielmann und ging seines Weges.   2.24

said the minstrel, and went his way.

Wiederum sprach er zu sich: 3.1

Again he said to himself:

»Zeit und Weile wird mir hier im Walde lang;   3.2

"I'm running out of time here in the forest;

ich will einen anderen Gesellen herbeiholen.«   3.3

I will fetch another journeyman."

nahm seine Geige und der Klang erschallte durch den
Wald.   3.4

He took his violin and the sound rang through the forest.

Da kam ein Häschen dahergesprungen. »Ach,   3.5

Then a rabbit came hopping along. "Oh,

ein Hase kommt!« sagte der Spielmann,   3.6

here comes a rabbit!" said the minstrel,

»den wollte ich nicht haben.«   3.7

"I didn't want him."

3.8 »Ei, du lieber Spielmann.« sagte das Häschen,
"Oh, dear minstrel." said the bunny,

3.9 »was fiedelst du so schön, das möchte ich auch lernen.«
"what a lovely fiddle you play, I'd like to learn that too."

3.10 »Das ist bald gelernt.« sprach der Spielmann,
"That will soon be learned." said the minstrel,

3.11 »du mußt nur alles thun, was ich dich heiße.«
"you must only do everything I bid you."

3.12 »O Spielmann.« antwortete das Häslein,
"O minstrel." answered the little rabbit,

3.13 »ich will dir gehorchen wie ein Schüler seinem Meister.«
"I will obey you as a pupil obeys his master."

3.14 Sie gingen ein Stück Weges zusammen, bis sie zu einer lichten Stelle im Wald kamen, wo ein Espenbaum stand.
They walked a little way together, until they came to a bright spot in the forest where an aspen tree stood.

3.15 Der Spielmann band dem Häschen einen langen Bindfaden um den Hals, wovon er das andere Ende an den Baum knüpfte.
The minstrel tied a long piece of string around the bunny's neck and tied the other end to the tree.

3.16 »Munter, Häschen, jetzt spring mir zwanzigmal an dem Baum herum.«
"Cheer up, bunny, now jump around the tree twenty times."

rief der Spielmann, und das Häschen gehorchte, und 3.17
wie es zwanzigmal herumgelaufen war, so hatte
sich der Bindfaden zwanzigmal um den Stamm
gewickelt und das Häschen war gefangen, und es
mochte ziehen und zerren wie es wollte, es schnitt
sich nur der Faden in den weichen Hals.

called the minstrel, and the bunny obeyed, and as it had
run around twenty times, the string had wrapped itself
around the trunk twenty times and the bunny was caught,
and it could pull and tug as much as it wanted, but the
string cut into its soft neck.

»Warte da so lange, bis ich wiederkomme.« 3.18

"Wait there until I come back."

sprach der Spielmann und ging weiter. 3.19

said the minstrel and went on his way.

Der Wolf indessen hatte gerückt, gezogen, an dem 4.1
Stein gebissen und so lange gearbeitet, bis er die
Pfoten frei gemacht und wieder aus der Spalte
gezogen hatte.

The wolf, meanwhile, had been pulling, tugging and biting
at the stone until he had freed his paws and pulled them out
of the crevice again.

Voll Zorn und Wut eilte er hinter dem Spielmann her 4.2
und wollte ihn zerreißen.

Full of anger and rage, he rushed after the minstrel and
wanted to tear him apart.

Als ihn der Fuchs laufen sah, 4.3

When the fox saw him running,

fing er an zu jammern und schrie aus Leibeskräften: 4.4

he began to wail and screamed at the top of his lungs:

4.5 »Bruder Wolf, komm mir zur Hilfe, der Spielmann hat mich betrogen.«

"Brother wolf, come to my aid, the minstrel has betrayed me."

4.6 Der Wolf zog die Bäumchen herab, biß die Schnüre entzwei und machte den Fuchs frei, der mit ihm ging und an dem Spielmann Rache nehmen wollte.

The wolf pulled down the little trees, broke the strings in two and freed the fox, who went with him and wanted to take revenge on the minstrel.

4.7 Sie fanden das gebundene Häschen, das sie ebenfalls erlösten, und dann suchten alle zusammen ihren Feind auf.

They found the tied bunny, which they also released, and then they all went together to find their enemy.

5.1 Der Spielmann hatte auf seinem Wege abermals seine Fiedel erklingen lassen und diesmal war er glücklicher gewesen.

The minstrel had once again sounded his fiddle on his way and this time he had been luckier.

5.2 Die Töne drangen zu den Ohren eines armen Holzhauers, der alsbald, er mochte wollen oder nicht, von der Arbeit abließ, und mit dem Beil unter dem Arme herankam, die Musik zu hören.

The sound reached the ears of a poor woodcutter, who, whether he wanted to or not, immediately left his work and came to listen to the music with his axe under his arm.

5.3 »Endlich kommt doch der rechte Geselle.«

"At last the right fellow has come."

5.4 sagte der Spielmann,

said the minstrel,

»denn einen Menschen suchte ich und keine wilden Tiere.« 5.5

"for I was looking for a man and not wild beasts."

Und fing an und spielte so schön und lieblich, daß der arme Mann wie bezaubert dastand und ihm das Herz vor Freude aufging. 5.6

And he began, and played so beautifully and sweetly that the poor man stood there as if enchanted, and his heart was filled with joy.

Und wie er so stand, kamen der Wolf, der Fuchs und das Häslein heran, und er merkte wohl, daß sie etwas Böses im Schilde führten. 5.7

And as he stood thus, the wolf, the fox, and the little hare approached, and he perceived that they were up to some mischief.

Da erhob er seine blinkende Axt und stellte sich vor den Spielmann, als wollte er sagen: 5.8

Then he raised his flashing axe and stood before the minstrel, as if to say,

»Wer an ihn will, der hüte sich, der hat es mit mir zu thun.« 5.9

"Whoever wants to get at him, beware, he has to deal with me."

Da ward den Tieren angst und liefen in den Wald zurück, 5.10

The animals were frightened and ran back into the forest,

der Spielmann aber spielte dem Manne noch eins zum Dank und zog dann weiter. 5.11

but the minstrel played the man a thank-you song and then went on his way.

Der Teufel mit den drei goldenen Haaren

The Devil with the Three Golden Hairs

1.1 Es war einmal eine arme Frau, die gebar ein Söhnlein, und weil es eine Glückshaut um hatte, als es zur Welt kam, so ward ihm geweissagt, es werde im vierzehnten Jahre die Tochter des Königs zur Frau haben.

Once upon a time there was a poor woman who gave birth to a little son, and because he had a lucky skin on when he was born, it was prophesied that in his fourteenth year he would have the King's daughter to wife.

1.2 Es trug sich zu, daß der König bald darauf ins Dorf kam, und niemand wußte, daß es der König war, und als er die Leute fragte, was es Neues gäbe, so antworteten sie:

It happened that the King soon afterward came to the village, and no one knew that it was the King, and when he asked the people what news there was, they answered,

1.3 »Es ist in diesen Tagen ein Kind mit einer Glückshaut geboren;

"A child with a lucky skin has been born these days;

was so einer unternimmt, das schlägt ihm zum Glück
aus.

1.4

whatever such a one undertakes will be lucky for him.

Es ist ihm auch vorausgesagt, in seinem vierzehnten
Jahre solle er die Tochter des Königs zur Frau haben.«

1.5

It is also foretold that in his fourteenth year he shall have
the king's daughter to wife."

Der König, der ein böses Herz hatte und über die
Weissagungen sich ärgerte, ging zu den Eltern, that
ganz freundlich und sagte:

1.6

The King, who had an evil heart and was angry at the
prophecies, went to the parents, acted very kindly, and
said,

»Ihr armen Leute, überlaßt mir euer Kind, ich will es
versorgen.«

1.7

"You poor people, leave your child to me, I will take care of
it."

Anfangs weigerten sie sich, da aber der fremde Mann
schweres Geld dafür bot und sie dachten,

1.8

At first they refused, but as the strange man offered heavy
money for it, and they thought,

»Es ist ein Glückskind,

1.9

"It is a lucky child,

es muß doch zu seinem Besten ausschlagen.«

1.10

it must turn out for his good."

so willigten sie endlich ein und gaben ihm das Kind.

1.11

they at last consented and gave him the child.

2.1 **Der König legte es in eine Schachtel und ritt damit weiter, bis er zu einem tiefen Wasser kam:**

The king put it in a box and rode on with it until he came to a deep water:

2.2 **da warf er die Schachtel hinein und dachte:**

then he threw the box into it and thought:

2.3 **»Von dem unerwarteten Freier habe ich meine Tochter geholfen.«**

"I have helped my daughter from the unexpected suitor."

2.4 **Die Schachtel aber ging nicht unter, sondern schwamm wie ein Schiffchen, und es drang auch kein Tröpfchen Wasser hinein.**

But the box did not sink, but floated like a boat, and not a drop of water entered it.

2.5 **So schwamm sie bis zwei Meilen Von des Königs Hauptstadt, wo eine Mühle war, an dessen Wehr sie hängen blieb.**

So it floated as far as two miles from the king's capital, where there was a mill on whose weir it got stuck.

2.6 **Ein Mahlbursche, der glücklicherweise da stand und sie bemerkte, zog sie mit einem Haken heran und meinte große Schätze zu finden?**

A miller's boy, who was fortunately standing there and noticed her, drew her up with a hook, and thought he found great treasures?

2.7 **als er sie aber aufmachte, lag ein schöner Knabe darin, der ganz frisch und munter war.**

but when he opened her, there was a beautiful boy lying in her, who was quite fresh and lively.

Er brachte ihn zu den Müllersleuten, und weil diese keine Kinder hatten, freuten sie sich und sprachen,

2.8

He took him to the millers, and as they had no children, they rejoiced and said,

»Gott hat es uns beschert.«

2.9

"God has given it to us."

Sie pflegten den Findling wohl, und er wuchs in allen Tugenden heran.

2.10

They took good care of the foundling and he grew up in all his virtues.

Es trug sich zu, daß der König einmal bei einem Gewitter in die Mühle trat und die Müllersleute fragte, ob der große Junge ihr Sohn wäre.

3.1

It so happened that the king once entered the mill during a thunderstorm and asked the millers if the big boy was their son.

»Nein.« antworteten sie,

3.2

"No." they replied,

»es ist ein Findling, er ist vor vierzehn Jahren in einer Schachtel ans Wehr geschwommen, und der Mahlbursche hat ihn aus dem Wasser gezogen.«

3.3

"it's a foundling, he floated to the weir in a box fourteen years ago, and the miller's boy pulled him out of the water."

Da merkte der König, daß es niemand anders als das Glückskind war, das er ins Wasser geworfen hatte, und sprach:

3.4

Then the King realized that it was none other than the lucky boy whom he had thrown into the water, and said,

3.5 »Ihr guten Leute, könnte der Junge nicht einen Brief an die Frau Königin bringen, ich will ihm zwei Goldstücke zum Lohn geben?«

"Good people, could not the boy bring a letter to the Queen, and I will give him two pieces of gold as a reward?"

3.6 »Wie der Herr König gebietet.« antworteten die Leute,

"As the King commands." answered the people,

3.7 und hießen den Jungen sich bereit halten.

and bade the boy be ready.

3.8 Da schrieb der König einen Brief an die Königin, worin stand:

Then the king wrote a letter to the queen, saying:

3.9 »Sobald der Knabe mit diesem Schreiben angelangt ist, soll er getötet und begraben werden, und das alles soll geschehen sein, ehe ich zurückkomme.«

"As soon as the boy has arrived with this letter, he shall be killed and buried, and all this shall be done before I return."

4.1 Der Knabe machte sich mit diesem Brief auf den Weg,

The boy set off with this letter,

4.2 verirrte sich aber und kam abends in einen großen Wald.

but got lost and came to a large forest in the evening.

4.3 In, der Dunkelheit sah er ein kleines Licht, ging darauf zu und gelangte zu einem Häuschen.

In the darkness he saw a small light, walked towards it and came to a little house.

4.4 Als er hineintrat,

When he went inside,

saß eine alte Frau beim Feuer ganz allein.   4.5
an old woman was sitting by the fire all alone.

Sie erschrak, als sie den Knaben erblickte und sprach: 4.6
She was startled when she saw the boy and said:

»Wo kommst du her und wo willst du hin?«   4.7
"Where have you come from and where are you going?"

»Ich komme von der Mühle.« antwortete er,   4.8
"I have come from the mill." he answered,

»und will zur Frau Königin, der ich einen Brief   4.9
bringen soll;
"and I want to go to the Queen, to whom I am to bring a
letter;

weil ich mich aber in dem Walde verirrt habe,   4.10
but as I have lost my way in the forest,

so wollte ich hier gern übernachten. «, »Du armer   4.11
Junge.«
I would like to spend the night here. ", "You poor boy."

sprach die Frau,   4.12
said the woman,

»du bist in ein Räuberhaus geraten, und wenn sie   4.13
heim kommen, so bringen sie dich um.«
"you have fallen into a robber's house, and when they come
home they will kill you."

»Mag kommen wer will.« sagte der Junge,   4.14
"Come who will." said the boy,

»ich fürchte mich nicht;   4.15
"I am not afraid;

4.16 ich bin aber so müde, daß ich nicht weiter kann.«
but I am so tired that I can go no farther."

4.17 streckte sich auf eine Bank und schlief ein.
He stretched himself on a bench and fell asleep.

4.18 Bald hernach kamen die Räuber und fragten zornig, was da für ein fremder Knabe läge.
Soon afterward the robbers came and asked angrily what strange boy was lying there.

4.19 »Ach.« sagte die Alte,
"Ah." said the old woman,

4.20 »es ist ein unschuldiges Kind, es hat sich im Walde verirrt, und ich habe es aus Barmherzigkeit aufgenommen:
"it is an innocent child, it has lost its way in the forest, and I have taken it in out of mercy:

4.21 es soll einen Brief an die Frau Königin bringen.«
it is to bring a letter to the Queen."

4.22 Die Räuber erbrachen den Brief und lasen ihn, und es stand darin, daß der Knabe sogleich, wie er ankäme, sollte ums Leben gebracht werden.
The robbers broke open the letter and read it, and it said that the boy was to be put to death as soon as he arrived.

Da empfanden die hartherzigen Räuber Mitleid, und   4.23
der Anführer zerriß den Brief und schrieb einen
anderen, und es stand darin, so wie der Knabe
ankäme, sollte er sogleich mit der Königstochter
vermählt werden.
Then the hard-hearted robbers felt pity, and the leader
tore up the letter and wrote another, and it said that as
soon as the boy arrived he should be married to the King's
daughter.

Sie ließen ihn dann ruhig bis zum anderen Morgen   4.24
auf der Bank liegen, und als er aufgewacht war, gaben
sie ihm den Brief und zeigten ihm den rechten Weg.
They left him to lie quietly on the bench until the next
morning, and when he woke up, they gave him the letter
and showed him the right way.

Die Königin aber, als sie den Brief empfangen   4.25
und gelesen hatte, that wie darin stand, hieß
ein prächtiges Hochzeitsfest anstellen, und die
Königstochter ward mit dem, Glückskind, vermählt;
The Queen, however, when she had received and read the
letter, did as it said, and ordered a splendid wedding feast
to be arranged, and the King's daughter was married to the
lucky child;

und da der Jüngling schön und freundlich war,   4.26
and as the youth was handsome and kind,

so lebte sie vergnügt und zufrieden mit ihm.   4.27
she lived happily and contentedly with him.

Nach einiger Zeit kam der König wieder in sein   5.1
Schloß und sah,
After some time,

44

5.2 daß die Weissagung erfüllt und das Glückskind mit
seiner Tochter vermählt war.
the king returned to his castle and saw that the prophecy
had been fulfilled and that the lucky child had been
married to his daughter.

5.3 »Wie ist das zugegangen?« sprach er,
"How did this happen?" he said,

5.4 »ich habe in meinem Brief einen ganz anderen Befehl
erteilt.«
"I gave a very different order in my letter."

5.5 Da reichte ihm die Königin den Brief und sagte, er
möchte selbst sehen was darin stände.
Then the queen handed him the letter and said that he
might see for himself what it said.

5.6 Der König las den Brief und merkte wohl, daß er mit
einem anderen, war vertauscht worden.
The king read the letter and realized that it had been mixed
up with another.

5.7 Er fragte den Jüngling, wie es mit dem anvertrauten
Briefe zugegangen wäre, warum er einen anderen
dafür gebracht hätte.
He asked the youth what had happened to the entrusted
letter, why he had brought another one in its place.

5.8 »Ich weiß von nichts.« antwortete er,
"I know nothing." he replied,

5.9 »er muß mir in der Nacht vertauscht, sein, als ich im
Walde geschlafen habe.«
"it must have been exchanged for me in the night when I
was sleeping in the forest."

Voll Zorn sprach der König: 5.10
Full of anger, the king said,

»So leicht soll es dir nicht werden, wer meine Tochter   5.11
haben will, der muß mir aus der Hölle drei goldene
Haare von dem Haupte des Teufels holen; bringst
du mir was ich verlange, so sollst du meine Tochter
behalten.«
"It shall not be so easy for you; whoever wants my daughter
must fetch me from hell three golden hairs from the
devil's head; if you bring me what I ask, you shall keep
my daughter."

Damit hoffte der König ihn auf immer los zu werden.   5.12
With this the king hoped to be rid of him for ever.

Das Glückskind aber antwortete: 5.13
But the lucky child replied:

»Die goldenen Haare will ich wohl holen,   5.14
"I will fetch the golden hairs,

ich fürchte mich vor dem Teufel nicht.«   5.15
I am not afraid of the devil."

Darauf nahm er Abschied und begann seine   5.16
Wanderschaft.
He then took his leave and began his wanderings.

Der Weg führte ihn zu einer großen Stadt, wo ihn   6.1
der Wächter an dem Thore ausfragte, was für ein
Gewerbe er verstände und was er wüßte.
The path led him to a large town, where the guard at the
gate asked him what trade he knew and what he knew.

»Ich weiß alles.« antwortete das Glückskind.   6.2
"I know everything." replied the lucky child.

6.3 »So kannst du uns einen Gefallen thun.« sagte der Wächter,

"So you can do us a favor." said the guard,

6.4 »wenn du uns sagst, warum unser Marktbrunnen, aus dem sonst Wein quoll, trocken geworden ist, und nicht einmal mehr Wasser siebt.«

"if you tell us why our market fountain, from which wine used to flow, has gone dry and no longer even filters water."

6.5 »Das sollt ihr erfahren.« anwortete er,

"You shall find out." he replied,

6.6 »wartet nur bis ich wiederkomme.«

"just wait until I come back."

6.7 Da ging er weiter und kam vor eine andere Stadt, da fragte der Thorwächter wiederum, was für ein Gewerbe er verstünde und was er wüßte.

So he went on and came to another town, where the gatekeeper again asked what trade he knew and what he knew.

6.8 »Ich weiß alles!« antwortete er.

"I know everything!" he replied.

6.9 »So kannst du uns einen Gefallen thun und uns sagen, warum ein Baum in unserer Stadt, der sonst goldene Äpfel trug, jetzt nicht einmal Blätter hervortreibt.«

"So can you do us a favor and tell us why a tree in our town that used to bear golden apples now doesn't even produce leaves."

6.10 »Das sollt ihr erfahren.« antwortete er,

"You shall find out." he replied,

6.11 »wartet nur bis ich wiederkomme.«

"just wait until I come back."

Da ging er weiter, und kam an ein großes Wasser, über das er hinüber mußte.   6.12
Then he went on and came to a large body of water which he had to cross.

Der Fährmann fragte ihn, was er für ein Gewerbe verstände und was er wüßte.   6.13
The ferryman asked him what business he was in and what he knew.

»Ich weiß alles.« antwortete er.   6.14
"I know everything." he replied.

»So kannst du mir einen Gefallen thun.« sprach der Fährmann,   6.15
"So can you do me a favor." said the ferryman,

»und mir sagen, warum ich immer hin - und herfahren muß und niemals abgelöst werde?«   6.16
"and tell me why I always have to go back and forth and am never relieved?"

»Das sollst du erfahren.« antwortete er.   6.17
"You shall know." he replied.

»warte nur bis ich wiederkomme.«   6.18
"Just wait till I come back."

Als er über das Wasser hinüber war,   7.1
When he had crossed the water,

so fand er den Eingang zur Hölle.   7.2
he found the entrance to hell.

7.3 Es war schwarz und rußig darin, und der Teufel war nicht zu Hause, aber seine Ellermutter saß da in einem breiten Sorgenstuhl.

It was black and sooty in there, and the devil was not at home, but his ell mother was sitting there in a wide worry chair.

7.4 »Was willst du?« sprach sie zu ihm,

"What do you want?" she said to him,

7.5 sah aber gar nicht so böse aus.

but she didn't look so angry.

7.6 »Ich wollte gern drei goldene Haare von des Teufels Kopf.«

"I would like three golden hairs from the devil's head."

7.7 antwortete er, »sonst kann ich meine Frau nicht behalten.«

he replied, "otherwise I can't keep my wife."

7.8 »Das ist viel verlangt.« sagte sie,

"That's a lot to ask." she said,

7.9 »wenn der Teufel heim kommt und findet dich,

"if the devil comes home and finds you,

7.10 so geht dir's an den Kragen;

you're in for it;

7.11 aber du dauerst mich, ich will sehen, ob ich dir helfen kann.«

but you keep me, I'll see if I can help you."

7.12 Sie verwandelte ihn in eine Ameise und sprach,

She turned him into an ant and said,

»Kriech in meine Rockfalten, da bist du sicher.« 7.13
"Crawl into the folds of my skirt, you'll be safe there."

»Ja.« antwortete er, 7.14
"Yes." he replied,

»das ist schon gut aber drei Dinge möchte ich gern 7.15
noch wissen, warum ein Brunnen, aus dem sonst
Wein quoll, trocken geworden ist, jetzt nicht einmal
mehr Wasser giebt;
"that's all very well, but I would like to know three more
things: why a well that used to gush wine has dried up and
now no longer even gives water;

warum ein Baum, der sonst goldene Äpfel trug, nicht 7.16
einmal mehr Laub treibt, und warum ein Fährmann
immer herüber und hinüber fahren muß und nicht
abgelöst wird.«
why a tree that used to bear golden apples no longer even
sprouts leaves, and why a ferryman always has to go back
and forth and is never relieved."

»Das sind schwere Fragen.« antwortete sie, 7.17
"Those are hard questions." she answered,

»aber halte dich nur still und ruhig, und hab acht was 7.18
der Teufel spricht, wenn ich ihm die drei goldenen
Haare ausziehe.«
"but just keep still and quiet, and be careful what the devil
says when I pull out his three golden hairs."

Als der Abend einbrach, kam der Teufel nach Haus. 8.1
As evening fell, the devil came home.

Kaum war er eingetreten, so merkte er, daß die Luft 8.2
nicht rein war.
As soon as he entered, he realized that the air was not clean.

8.3 »Ich rieche, rieche Menschenfleisch.« sagte er,
"I smell, I smell human flesh." he said,

8.4 »es ist hier nicht richtig.«
"it's not right here."

8.5 Dann guckte er in alle Ecken und suchte,
Then he looked in every corner and searched,

8.6 konnte aber nichts finden. Die Ellermutter schalt ihn aus:
but could find nothing. The ell's mother scolded him:

8.7 »Eben ist erst gekehrt.« sprach sie,
"You've just swept up." she said,

8.8 »und alles in Ordnung gebracht,
"and put everything in order,

8.9 nun wirfst du mir's wieder untereinander:
now you're throwing it back in my face:

8.10 immer hast du Menschenfleisch in der Nase!
you always have human flesh in your nose!

8.11 Setze dich nieder und iß dein Abendbrot.«
Sit down and eat your supper."

8.12 Als er gegessen und getrunken hatte, war er müde, legte der Ellermutter seinen Kopf in den Schoß und sagte, sie sollte ihn ein wenig lausen.
When he had eaten and drunk, he was tired and laid his head in his ell's mother's lap and told her to give him a little rest.

Es dauerte nicht lange, so schlummerte er ein, blies
und schnarchte.

8.13

It was not long before he fell asleep, blew and snored.

Da faßte die Alte ein goldenes Haar,

8.14

Then the old woman grabbed a golden hair,

riß es aus und legte es neben sich. »Autsch!«

8.15

pulled it out and laid it beside her. "Ouch!"

schrie der Teufel, »was hast du vor?«

8.16

cried the devil, "what are you up to?"

»Ich habe einen schweren Traum gehabt.«

8.17

"I had a bad dream."

antwortete die Ellermutter,

8.18

replied the ellum mother,

»da hab ich dir in die Haare gefaßt.«

8.19

"I grabbed your hair."

»Was hat dir denn geträumt?« fragte der Teufel.

8.20

"What did you dream?" asked the devil.

»Mir hat geträumt, ein Marktbrunnen, aus dem sonst
Wein quoll, sei versiegt, und es habe nicht einmal
Wasser daraus quellen wollen, was ist wohl schuld
daran?«

8.21

"I dreamt that a market fountain, from which wine used
to flow, had dried up, and that water wouldn't even spring
from it, what do you think is to blame?"

»He, wenn sie's wüßten!« antwortete der Teufel,

8.22

"Hey, if you only knew!" replied the devil,

8.23 »es sitzt eine Kröte unter einem Stein im Brunnen, wenn sie die töten, so wird der Wein schon wieder fließen.«

"there's a toad sitting under a stone in the well, if you kill it, the wine will flow again."

8.24 Die Ellermutter lauste ihn wieder, bis er einschlief und schnarchte, daß die Fenster zitterten.

The ell's mother listened to him again until he fell asleep and snored so that the windows shook.

8.25 Da riß sie ihm das zweite Haar aus. »Hu!

Then she tore out his second hair. "Hoo!

8.26 was machst du?« schrie der Teufel zornig.

What are you doing?" cried the devil angrily.

8.27 »Nimm's nicht übel.« antwortete sie.

"Don't take offense." she replied.

8.28 »ich habe es im Traum gethan.«

"I did it in a dream."

8.29 »Was hat dir wieder geträumt?« fragte er.

"What did you dream again?" he asked.

8.30 »Mir hat geträumt, in einem Königreich stand ein Obstbaum, der hätte sonst goldene Äpfel getragen und wollte jetzt nicht einmal Laub treiben.

"I dreamt that there was a fruit tree in a kingdom that would otherwise have borne golden apples and now wouldn't even sprout leaves.

8.31 Was war wohl die Ursache davon?«

I wonder what caused that?"

8.32 »He, wenn sie's wüßten!« antwortete der Teufel,

"Hey, if they only knew!" replied the devil,

»an der Wurzel nagt eine Maus, wenn sie die töten, so wird er schon wieder goldene Äpfel tragen, nagt sie aber noch länger, so verdorrt der Baum gänzlich.

8.33

"A mouse is gnawing at the root, if they kill it, it will bear golden apples again, but if it gnaws any longer, the tree will wither away completely.

Aber laß mich mit deinen Träumen in Ruhe, wenn du mich noch einmal im Schlafe störst, so kriegst du eine Ohrfeige.«

8.34

But leave me alone with your dreams, if you disturb my sleep again, I'll slap you in the face."

Die Ellermutter sprach ihn gut zu,

8.35

The ellmother spoke well to him,

und lauste ihn wieder bis er eingeschlafen war und schnarchte.

8.36

and listened to him again until he fell asleep and snored.

Da faßte sie das dritte goldene Haar und riß es ihm aus.

8.37

Then she seized the third golden hair and tore it out.

Der Teufel fuhr in die Höhe, schrie und wollte übel mit ihr wirtschaften, aber sie besänftigte ihn nochmals und sprach,

8.38

The devil went up, screamed and wanted to do evil to her, but she soothed him again and said,

»Wer kann für böse Träume!«

8.39

"Who can be responsible for bad dreams!"

»Was hat dir denn geträumt?« fragte er, und war doch neugierig.

8.40

"What did you dream?" he asked, but he was still curious.

8.41 »Mir hat von einem Fährmann geträumt, der sich beklagte, daß er immer hin - und herfahren müßte, und nicht abgelöst würde.

"I dreamed of a ferryman who complained that he always had to go back and forth and was never relieved.

8.42 Was ist wohl schuld?«

What do you think is to blame?"

8.43 »He, der Dummbart!« antwortete der Teufel,

"Hey, the fool!" replied the devil,

8.44 »wenn einer kommt und will überfahren, so muß er ihm die Stange in die Hand geben, dann muß der andere überfahren und er ist frei.«

"if someone comes and wants to cross, he has to put the pole in his hand, then the other one has to cross and he is free."

8.45 Da die Ellermutter ihm die drei goldenen Haare ausgerissen hatte und die drei Fragen beantwortet waren, so ließ sie den alten Drachen in Ruhe, und er schlief bis der Tag anbrach.

When the Elf's mother had plucked out his three golden hairs and the three questions were answered, she left the old dragon alone, and he slept till daybreak.

9.1 Als der Teufel wieder fortgezogen war,

When the devil had gone away again,

9.2 holte die Alte die Ameise aus der Rockfalte und gab dem Glückskind die menschliche Gestalt zurück.

the old woman took the ant out of the fold of her skirt and gave the lucky child back his human form.

9.3 »Da hast du die drei goldenen Haare.« sprach sie,

"There you have the three golden hairs." she said,

»was der Teufel zu deinen drei Fragen gesagt hat, wirst du wohl gehört haben.«   9.4

"you must have heard what the devil said about your three questions."

»Ja.« antwortete er.   9.5

"Yes." he replied.

»ich habe es gehört und will's wohl behalten.«   9.6

"I have heard it, and I will keep it."

»So ist dir geholfen.« sagte sie,   9.7

"So you have been helped." she said,

»und nun kannst du deiner Wege ziehen.«   9.8

"and now you can go your way."

Er bedankte sich bei der Alten für die Hilfe in der Not, verließ die Hölle, und war vergnügt, daß ihm alles so wohl geglückt war.   9.9

He thanked the old woman for her help in his trouble, left hell, and was glad that everything had gone so well for him.

Als er zu dem Fährmann kam,   9.10

When he came to the ferryman,

sollte er ihm die versprochene Antwort geben.   9.11

he was to give him the promised answer.

»Fahr mich erst hinüber.« sprach das Glückskind,   9.12

"Drive me over first." said the lucky child,

»so will ich dir sagen, wie du erlöst wirst.«   9.13

"and I will tell you how you can be saved."

und als er auf dem jenseitigen Ufer angelangt war,   9.14

And when he had reached the other side of the river,

9.15 **gab er ihm des Teufels Rat:**
he gave him the devil's advice:

9.16 **»Wenn wieder einer kommt und will übergefahren sein,**
"If any one comes again and wants to be driven over,

9.17 **so gieb ihm nur die Stange in die Hand.«**
just give him the pole in his hand."

9.18 **Er ging weiter und kam zu der Stadt, worin der unfruchtbare Baum stand, und wo der Wächter auch Antwort haben wollte.**
He went on and came to the town where the barren tree stood, and where the watchman also wanted an answer.

9.19 **Da sagte er ihm, wie er vom Teufel gehört hatte:**
There he told him, as he had heard from the devil:

9.20 **»Tötet die Maus, die an seiner Wurzel nagt, so wird er wieder goldene Äpfel tragen.«**
"Kill the mouse that gnaws at its root and it will bear golden apples again."

9.21 **Da dankte ihm der Wächter und gab ihm zur Belohnung zwei mit Gold beladene Esel,**
Then the guard thanked him and gave him two donkeys laden with gold as a reward,

9.22 **die mußten ihm nachfolgen.**
and they had to follow him.

9.23 **Zuletzt kam er zu der Stadt, deren Brunnen versiegt war.**
At last he came to the city whose well had dried up.

Da sprach er zu dem Wächter, wie der Teufel
gesprochen hatte:

9.24

There he said to the watchman, as the devil had said:

»Es sitzt eine Kröte im Brunnen unter einem Stein,
die müßt ihr aufsuchen und töten, so wird er wieder
reichlich Wein geben.«

9.25

"There is a toad in the well under a stone, you must seek it
out and kill it, and it will give plenty of wine again."

Der Wächter dankte und gab ihm ebenfalls zwei mit
Gold beladene Esel.

9.26

The guard thanked him and also gave him two donkeys
laden with gold.

Endlich gelangte das Glückskind daheim bei seiner
Frau an,

10.1

At last the lucky child arrived home with his wife,

die sich herzlich freute als sie ihn wiedersah und
hörte wie wohl ihm alles gelungen war.

10.2

who was very happy when she saw him again and heard
how well everything had worked out for him.

Dem König brachte er was er verlangt hatte, die drei
goldenen Haare des Teufels, und als dieser die vier
Esel mit dem Golde sah, ward er ganz vergnügt und
sprach:

10.3

He brought the king what he had asked for, the devil's
three golden hairs, and when he saw the four donkeys with
the gold, he was delighted and said,

»Nun sind alle Bedingungen erfüllt und du kannst
meine Tochter behalten.

10.4

"Now all the conditions have been met and you can keep my
daughter.

10.5 Aber, lieber Schwiegersohn, sage mir doch, woher ist das viele Gold?

But, dear son-in-law, tell me, where is all this gold from?

10.6 Das sind ja gewaltige Schätze!«

These are tremendous treasures!"

10.7 »Ich bin über einen Fluß gefahren.« antwortete er,

"I crossed a river." he replied,

10.8 »und da habe ich es mitgenommen, es liegt dort statt des Sandes am Ufer.«

"and I took it with me and it's lying there on the bank instead of the sand."

10.9 »Kann ich mir auch davon holen?«

"Can I take some for myself?"

10.10 sprach der König und war ganz begierig.

said the king, eagerly.

10.11 »So viel Ihr nur wollt.« antwortete er,

"As much as you like." he answered,

10.12 »es ist ein Fährmann auf dem Fluß, von dem laßt Euch überfahren, so könnt Ihr drüben Eure Säcke füllen.«

"there is a ferryman on the river, let him take you across, and you can fill your sacks on the other side."

10.13 Der habsüchtige König machte sich in aller Eile auf den Weg, und als er zu dem Fluß kam, so winkte er dem Fährmann, der sollte ihn übersetzen.

The greedy king set off in all haste, and when he came to the river, he beckoned to the ferryman to take him across.

Der Fährmann kam und hieß ihn einsteigen, und   10.14
als sie an das jenseitige Ufer kamen, gab er ihm die
Ruderstange in die Hand und sprang davon.

The ferryman came and told him to get in, and when they
came to the other bank, he gave him the oar-pole in his
hand and jumped away.

Der König aber mußte von nun an fahren zur Strafe   10.15
für seine Sünden.

But the king had to sail from then on as punishment for his
sins.

»Fährt er wohl noch?«   11.1

"Is he still driving?"

»Was denn? es wird ihm niemand die Stange   11.2
abgenommen haben.«

"What is it? Nobody will have taken the bar from him."

Tischchen deck' dich, Goldesel, und Knüppel aus dem Sack

Lay the Table, Golden Donkey, and take the Cudgels out of the Bag

1.1 Vor alten Zeiten war ein Schneider, der drei Söhne hatte und nur eine einzige Ziege.

Once upon a time there was a tailor who had three sons and only one goat.

1.2 Aber die Ziege, weil sie alle zusammen mit ihrer Milch ernährte, mußte ihr gutes Futter haben und täglich hinaus auf die Weide geführt werden.

But the goat, because it fed them all with its milk, had to have good food and be taken out to pasture every day.

1.3 Die Söhne thaten das auch nach der Reihe.

The sons did this in turn.

1.4 Einmal brachte sie der älteste auf den Kirchhof, wo die schönsten Kräuter standen, ließ sie da fressen und herumspringen.

Once the eldest took her to the churchyard, where the most beautiful herbs grew, and let her eat and jump around.

Abends, als es Zeit war heim zu gehen, fragte er: 1.5

In the evening, when it was time to go home, he asked:

»Ziege, bist du satt?« Die Ziege antwortete: 1.6

"Goat, are you full?" The goat replied:

»Ich bin so satt,	"I'm so full,
ich mag kein Blatt: meh! meh!«	I don't like leaves: meh! meh!"

»So komm nach Hause.«   "So come home."   3.1

sprach der Junge, faßte sie am Strickchen, führte sie in den Stall und band sie fest.   said the boy, taking her by the rope, leading her into the stable and tying her up.   3.2

»Nun.« sagte der alte Schneider,   "Well." said the old tailor,   3.3

»hat die Ziege ihr gehöriges Futter?«   "has the goat had her proper food?"   3.4

»O.« antwortete der Sohn,   "Oh." replied the son,   3.5

»die ist so satt, sie mag kein Blatt.«   "she's so full she doesn't like leaves."   3.6

Der Vater aber wollte sich selber überzeugen, ging hinab in den Stall, streichelte das liebe Tier und fragte: But the father wanted to see for himself, went down to the stable, stroked the dear animal and asked: 3.7

»Ziege, bist du auch satt?« Die Ziege antwortete: "Goat, are you full too?" The goat replied: 3.8

62

»Wovon sollt ich satt sein?

"What should I be full of?

ich sprang nur über Gräbelein,

I only jumped over small ditches,

und fand kein einzig Blättelein: meh! meh!«

and found not a single leaf: meh! meh!"

5.1 »Was muß ich hören!«

"What must I hear!"

5.2 rief der Schneider, lief hinauf und sprach zu dem Jungen:

cried the tailor, and ran up and said to the boy,

5.3 »Ei, du Lügner, sagst, die Ziege wäre satt, und hast sie hungern lassen?«

"Why, you liar, you say the goat is full, and have let her go hungry?"

5.4 und in seinem Zorn nahm er die Elle von der Wand und jagte ihn mit Schlägen hinaus.

and in his anger he took the yard-arm from the wall and chased him out with blows.

6.1 Am anderen Tage war die Reihe am zweiten Sohn, der suchte an der Gartenhecke einen Platz aus, wo lauter gute Kräuter standen und die Ziege fraß sie rein ab.

The next day, it was the second son's turn; he picked a place in the garden hedge where there were lots of good herbs and the goat ate them clean.

6.2 Abends, als er heim wollte, fragte er: »Ziege,

In the evening, when he wanted to go home, he asked: "Goat,

6.3 bist du satt?« Die Ziege antwortete:

are you full?" The goat replied:

»Ich bin so satt,	"I'm so full,	
ich mag kein Blatt: meh! meh!«	I don't like leaves: meh! meh!"	
»So komm nach Haus.« sprach der Junge,	"So come home." said the boy,	8.1
zog sie heim und band sie im Stall fest. »Nun.«	pulling her home and tying her up in the stable. "Well."	8.2
sagte, der alte Schneider,	said the old tailor,	8.3
»hat die Ziege ihr gehöriges Futter?«	"has the goat had her proper food?"	8.4
»O.« antwortete der Sohn,	"Oh." replied the son,	8.5
»die ist so satt, sie mag kein Blatt.«	"she's so full she doesn't like leaves."	8.6
Der Schneider wollte sich darauf nicht verlassen, ging hinab in den Stall und fragte,	The tailor would not rely on this, and went down to the stable and asked,	8.7
»Ziege, bist du auch satt?« Die Ziege antwortete:	"Goat, are you full too?" The goat replied:	8.8
»Wovon sollt ich satt sein?	"What should I be full of?	
ich sprang nur über Gräbelein,	I only jumped over small ditches,	

und fand kein einzig Blättelein: meh! meh!«

and found not a single leaf: meh! meh!"

10.1

»Der gottlose Bösewicht!« schrie der Schneider,

"The godless villain!" cried the tailor,

10.2

»so ein frommes Tier hungern zu lassen!«

"to let such a pious animal go hungry!"

10.3

lief hinauf und schlug mit der Elle den Jungen zur Hausthür hinaus.

he ran up and beat the boy out of the house with his crook.

11.1 Die Reihe kam jetzt an den dritten Sohn, der wollte seine Sache gut machen, suchte Buschwerk mit dem schönsten Laube aus und ließ die Ziege daran fressen.

The turn now came to the third son, who wanted to do his job well, picked out some bushes with the most beautiful foliage and let the goat eat them.

11.2 Abends, als er heim wollte, fragte er: »Ziege,

In the evening, when he wanted to go home, he asked: "Goat,

11.3 bist du auch satt?« Die Ziege antwortete:

are you full too?" The goat replied:

»Ich bin so satt,

"I'm so full,

ich mag kein Blatt: meh! meh!«

I don't like leaves: meh! meh!"

13.1

»So komm nach Haus.« sagte der Junge,

"So come home." said the boy,

65

führte sie in den Stall und band sie fest. »Nun.«	leading her into the stable and tying her up. "Well."	13.2
sagte der alte Schneider,	said the old tailor,	13.3
»hat die Ziege ihr gehöriges Futter?«	"has the goat had her proper food?"	13.4
»O.« antwortete der Sohn,	"Oh." replied the son,	13.5
»die ist so satt, sie mag kein Blatt.«	"she's so full she doesn't like leaves."	13.6
Der Schneider traute nicht, ging hinab und fragte: »Ziege,	The tailor did not trust him, went down and asked, "Goat,	13.7
bist du auch satt?« Das boshafte Tier antwortete:	are you full too?" The mischievous animal replied:	13.8
»Wovon sollt ich satt sein?	"What should I be full of?	
ich sprang nur über Gräbelein,	I only jumped over little ditches,	
und fand kein einzig Blättelein: meh! meh!«	and found not a single leaf: meh! meh!"	
»O die Lügenbrut!« rief der Schneider,	"Oh, the brood of liars!" cried the tailor,	15.1
»einer so gottlos und pflichtvergessen wie der andere!	"one as godless and as dutiful as the other!	15.2

15.3 Ihr sollt mich nicht länger zum Narren haben!«

You shall have me for a fool no longer!"

15.4 und vor Zorn ganz außer sich, sprang er hinauf und gerbte dem armen Jungen mit der Elle den Rücken so gewaltig, daß er zum Hause hinaussprang.

and quite beside himself with rage, he jumped up and rubbed the poor boy's back with his cubit so violently that he jumped out of the house.

16.1 Der alte Schneider war nun mit seiner Ziege allein.

The old tailor was now alone with his goat.

16.2 Am anderen Morgen ging er hinab in den Stall,

The next morning he went down to the stable,

16.3 liebkoste die Ziege und sprach:

caressed the goat and said:

16.4 »Komm, mein liebes Tierlein, ich will dich selbst zur Weide führen.«

"Come, my dear little animal, I will lead you to pasture myself."

16.5 Er nahm sie am Strick und brachte sie zu grünen Hecken und unter Schafrippe und was sonst die Ziegen gern fressen.

He took her by the rope and led her to green hedges and under sheep's ribs and whatever else goats like to eat.

16.6 »Da kannst du dich einmal nach Herzenslust sättigen.«

"There you can eat to your heart's content."

16.7 sprach er zu ihr, und ließ sie weiden bis zum Abend.

he said to her, and let her graze until evening.

Da fragte er: »Ziege, bist du satt?« Sie antwortete: 16.8
Then he asked: "Goat, are you full?" She replied:

»Ich bin so satt,   "I'm so full,

ich mag kein Blatt: meh!   I don't like leaves: meh!
meh!«   meh!"

»So komm nach Hause.«   "So come home." said   18.1
sagte der Schneider,   the tailor,

führte sie in den Stall   leading her into the   18.2
und band sie fest. Als er   stable and tying her up.
wegging,   As he left,

kehrte er sich noch einmal   he turned back and said: 18.3
um und sagte:

»Nun bist du doch einmal   "Now you've had   18.4
satt!«   enough!"

Aber die Ziege machte es   But the goat did him no   18.5
ihm nicht besser und rief: better and called out:

»Wie sollt ich satt sein?   "How am I supposed to
                                      be full?

ich sprang nur über   I only jumped over small
Gräbelein,   ditches,

und fand kein einzig   and found not a single
Blättelein: meh! meh!«   leaf: meh! meh!"

68

20.1 Als der Schneider das hörte, stutzte er und sah wohl, daß er seine drei Söhne ohne Ursache verstoßen hatte.

When the tailor heard this, he was taken aback and realized that he had rejected his three sons without cause.

20.2 »Wart.« rief er,

"Wait." he cried,

20.3 »du undankbares Geschöpf, dich fortzujagen ist noch zu wenig, ich will dich zeichnen, daß du dich unter ehrbaren Schneidern nicht mehr darfst sehen lassen.«

"you ungrateful creature, to drive you away is still too little, I will mark you so that you may no longer be seen among respectable tailors."

20.4 In einer Hast sprang er hinauf, holte sein Bartmesser, seifte der Ziege den Kopf ein und schor sie so glatt wie seine flache Hand.

In a hurry he jumped up, fetched his beard-knife, soaped the goat's head and shaved it as smooth as his flat hand.

20.5 Und weil die Elle zu ehrenvoll gewesen wäre, holte er die Peitsche und versetzte ihr solche Hiebe, daß sie in gewaltigen Sprüngen davonlief.

And because the ell would have been too honorable, he fetched the whip and gave it such blows that it ran away in mighty leaps.

21.1 Der Schneider, als er so ganz einsam in seinem Hause saß, verfiel in große Traurigkeit und hätte seine Söhne gern wieder gehabt, aber niemand wußte wo sie hingeraten waren.

The tailor, as he sat so lonely in his house, fell into great sadness and would have liked to have his sons back, but no one knew where they had gone.

Der älteste war zu einem Schreiner in die Lehre   21.2
gegangen, da lernte er fleißig und unverdrossen,
und als seine Zeit herum war, daß er wandern sollte,
schenkte ihm der Meister ein Tischchen, das gar kein
besonderes Ansehen hatte und von gewöhnlichem
Holz war;

The eldest had been apprenticed to a carpenter, where he
learned diligently and undauntedly, and when it was time
for him to go away, the master gave him a little table, which
had no particular reputation and was made of ordinary
wood;

aber es hatte eine gute Eigenschaft.   21.3

but it had one good quality.

Wenn man es hinstellte und sprach: »Tischchen,   21.4
deck dich.«

When he set it down, and said, "Set the table."

so war das gute Tischchen auf einmal mit einem   21.5
sauberen Tüchlein bedeckt, und stand da ein Teller
und Messer und Gabel daneben, und Schüsseln mit
Gesottenem und Gebratenem, so viel Platz hatten,
und ein großes Glas mit rotem Wein leuchtete, daß
einem das Herz lachte.

the good little table was suddenly covered with a clean
cloth, and there stood a plate and knife and fork beside it,
and bowls of boiled and roasted food as much as would fit,
and a large glass of red wine shone so brightly that it made
one's heart smile.

Der junge Gesell dachte: »Damit hast du genug für   21.6
dein Lebtag.«

The young fellow thought, "That's enough for your life."

21.7 zog guter Dinge in der Welt umher und bekümmerte sich gar nicht darum, ob ein Wirtshaus gut oder schlecht und ob etwas darin zu finden war oder nicht.

and went about the world in good spirits, not caring at all whether an inn was good or bad, or whether there was anything to be found in it or not.

21.8 Wenn es ihm gefiel, so kehrte er garnicht ein, sondern im Felde, im Wald, aus einer Wiese, wo er Lust hatte, nahm er sein Tischchen vom Rücken, stellte es vor sich und sprach:

If he liked it, he did not stop at all, but in the field, in the forest, in a meadow, wherever he felt like it, he took his little table from his back, put it in front of him and said,

21.9 »Deck dich.« so war alles da, was sein Herz begehrte.

"Cover yourself." and there was everything his heart desired.

21.10 Endlich kam es ihm in den, Sinn, er wollte zu seinem Vater zurückkehren, sein Zorn würde, sich gelegt haben, und mit dem Tischen deck dich würde er ihn gern wieder aufnehmen.

At last it came into his head that he wanted to return to his father; his anger would have subsided, and with the table laid for him he would gladly receive him again.

21.11 Es trug sich zu, daß er auf dem Heimwege abends in ein Wirtshaus kam, das mit Gästen angefüllt war;

It so happened that on his way home in the evening he came to an inn which was full of guests;

21.12 sie hießen ihn willkommen und luden ihn ein, sich zu ihnen zu setzen und mit ihnen zu essen, sonst würde er schwerlich noch etwas bekommen.

they welcomed him and invited him to sit down and eat with them, otherwise he would hardly get anything else.

»Nein.« antwortete der Schreiner,   21.13

"No." replied the carpenter,

»die paar Bissen will ich euch nicht vor dem Munde   21.14
nehmen,

"I don't want to take a few bites from your mouths,

lieber sollt ihr meine Gäste sein.«   21.15

I'd rather you were my guests."

Sie lachten und meinten, er triebe seinen Spaß mit   21.16
ihnen.

They laughed and thought he was having fun with them.

Er aber stellte sein hölzernes Tischchen mitten in die   21.17
Stube und sprach:

But he placed his wooden table in the middle of the room
and said:

»Tischchen, deck dich.«   21.18

"Set the table."

Augenblicklich war es mit Speisen besetzt, so gut wie   21.19
sie der Wirt nicht hätte herbeischaffen können, und
wovon der Geruch den Gästen lieblich in die Nase
stieg.

In an instant, it was covered with food that the innkeeper
could not have brought, the smell of which filled the guests'
noses.

»Zugegriffen, liebe Freunde.«   21.20

"Take a bite, dear friends."

21.21 sprach der Schreiner, und die Gäste, als sie sahen, wie es gemeint war, ließen sie sich nicht zweimal bitten, rückten heran, zogen ihre Messer und griffen tapfer zu.

said the carpenter, and the guests, when they saw what was meant, did not need to be asked twice, moved closer, drew their knives and bravely took a bite.

21.22 Und was sie am meisten verwunderte, wenn eine Schüssel leer geworden war, so stellte sich gleich von selbst eine volle an ihren Platz.

And what surprised them most of all was that when a bowl was empty, a full one would immediately take its place.

21.23 Der Wirt stand in einer Ecke und sah dem Dinge zu;

The landlord stood in a corner and watched;

21.24 er wußte gar nicht was er sagen sollte, dachte aber:

he didn't know what to say, but thought:

21.25 »Einen solchen Koch könntest du in deiner Wirtschaft wohl brauchen.«

"You could do with a cook like that in your restaurant."

21.26 Der Schreiner und seine Gesellschaft waren lustig bis in die späte Nacht, endlich legten sie sich schlafen, und der junge Geselle ging auch zu Bett und stellte sein Wünschtischchen an die Wand.

The carpenter and his companions were merry till late at night, and at last they went to bed, and the young journeyman also went to bed and put his little table against the wall.

Dem Wirte aber ließen seine Gedanken keine Ruhe,   21.27
es fiel ihm ein, daß in seiner Rumpelkammer ein altes
Tischchen stände, das gerade so aussähe;
But the landlord's thoughts left him no peace, and it
occurred to him that there was an old table in his junk-
room which looked just like it;

das holte er ganz sachte herbei und vertauschte es   21.28
mit dem Wünschtischchen.
he brought it over very gently and exchanged it for the
wishing-table.

Am anderen Morgen zahlte der Schreiner sein   21.29
Schlafgeld, packte sein Tischchen auf, dachte, gar
nicht daran, daß er ein falsches hätte und ging seiner
Wege.
The next morning the carpenter paid his bed-money,
picked up his little table, thought nothing of having a
false one, and went his way.

Zu Mittag kam er bei seinem Vater an,   21.30
At noon he arrived at his father's house,

der ihn mit großer Freude empfing.   21.31
who received him with great joy.

»Nun, mein lieber Sohn, was hast du gelernt?« sagte   21.32
er zu ihm.
"Well, my dear son, what have you learned?" he said to
him.

»Vater, ich bin ein Schreiner geworden.«   21.33
"Father, I have become a carpenter."

»Ein gutes Handwerk.« erwiderte der Alte,   21.34
"A good trade." replied the old man,

21.35 »aber was hast du von deiner Wanderschaft mitgebracht?«

"but what have you brought back from your wanderings?"

21.36 »Vater, das beste, was ich mitgebracht habe, ist das Tischchen.«

"Father, the best thing I've brought back is the little table."

21.37 Der Schneider betrachtete es von allen Seiten und sagte,

The tailor looked at it from all sides and said,

21.38 »Daran hast du kein Meisterstück gemacht,

"You haven't made a masterpiece on it,

21.39 das ist ein altes und schlechtes Tischchen.«

it's an old and poor table."

21.40 »Aber es ist ein Tischchen deck dich.« antwortete der Sohn,

"But it is a little table." replied the son,

21.41 »wenn ich es hinstelle und sage ihm, es soll sich decken, so stehen gleich die schönsten Gerichte darauf und ein Wein dabei, der das Herz erfreut.

"if I put it down and tell it to set itself, it will immediately have the most beautiful dishes on it and a wine that delights the heart.

21.42 Ladet nur alle Verwandten und Freunde ein, die sollen sich einmal laben und erquicken, denn das Tischchen macht sie alle satt.«

Invite all your relatives and friends, and let them feast and refresh themselves, for this little table will satisfy them all."

Als die Gesellschaft beisammen war, stellte er sein
Tischchen mitten in die Stube und sprach,   21.43

When the company had gathered, he placed his little table
in the middle of the room and said,

»Tischchen, deck dich.«   21.44

"Set the table."

Aber das Tischchen regte sich nicht und blieb so leer
wie ein anderer Tisch, der die Sprache nicht versteht.   21.45

But the little table did not move and remained as empty as
another table that does not understand language.

Da merkte der arme Geselle, daß ihm das Tischchen
vertauscht war und schämte sich, daß er wie ein
Lügner dastand.   21.46

Then the poor journeyman realized that his little table had
been changed, and was ashamed to look like a liar.

Die Verwandten aber lachten ihn aus und mußten
ungetrunken und ungegessen wieder heim wandern.   21.47

But the relatives laughed at him and had to go home again
without drinking or eating.

Der Vater holte seine Lappen wieder herbei und
schneiderte fort,   21.48

The father fetched his rags again and went away to tailor,

der Sohn aber ging bei einem Meister in die Arbeit.   21.49

but the son went to work for a master.

Der zweite Sohn war zu einem Müller gekommen und
bei ihm in die Lehre gegangen.   22.1

The second son had come to a miller and was apprenticed to
him.

22.2 Als er seine Jahre herum hatte, sprach der Meister:
When he had completed his years, the master said:

22.3 »Weil du dich so wohl gehalten hast, so schenke ich dir einen Esel von einer besonderen Art, er zieht nicht am Wagen und trägt auch keine Säcke.«
"Because you have done so well, I am giving you a donkey of a special kind; it does not pull the cart and does not carry sacks."

22.4 »Wozu ist er denn nütze?« fragte der junge Geselle.
"What's it good for?" asked the young journeyman.

22.5 »Er speit Gold.« antwortete der Müller;
"He spits out gold." replied the miller;

22.6 »wenn du ihn auf ein Tuch stellst und sprichst: ›Bricklebrit,‹
"if you put him on a piece of cloth and say, 'Bricklebrit,'

22.7 so speit dir das gute Tier Goldstücke aus,
the good animal will spit out pieces of gold for you,

22.8 hinten und vorn.«
back and front."

22.9 »Das ist eine schöne Sache.« sprach der Geselle,
"That's a fine thing." said the journeyman,

22.10 dankte dem Meister und zog in die Welt.
thanked the master and went out into the world.

22.11 Wenn er Gold nötig hatte; brauchte er nur zu seinem Esel
If he needed gold, he only had to say

22.12 »Bricklebrit«
"Bricklebrit"

zu sagen, so regnete es Goldstücke, und er hatte
weiter keine Mühe als sie von der Erde aufzuheben.

22.13

to his donkey and it rained gold pieces, and he had no more
trouble than to pick them up from the ground.

Wo er hinkam, war ihm das beste gut genug, und je
teurer je lieber, denn er hatte immer einen vollen
Beutel.

22.14

Wherever he went, the best was good enough for him, and
the more expensive the better, for he always had a full bag.

Als er sich eine Zeitlang in der Welt umgesehen hatte,
dachte er:

22.15

When he had looked about the world for some time, he
thought,

»Du mußt deinen Vater aufsuchen, wenn du mit dem
Goldesel kommst, so wird er seinen Zorn vergessen
und dich gut aufnehmen.«

22.16

"You must go and see your father, if you come with the gold
ass, he will forget his anger and receive you well."

Es trug sich zu, daß er in dasselbe Wirtshaus geriet,
in welchem seinem Bruder das Tischchen vertauscht
war.

22.17

It so happened that he came to the same inn where his
brother's little table had been exchanged.

Er führte seinen Esel an der Hand und der Wirt
wollte ihm das Tier abnehmen und anbinden, der
junge Geselle aber sprach:

22.18

He led his donkey by the hand, and the innkeeper wanted
to take the animal from him and tie it up, but the young
journeyman said,

22.19 »Gebt Euch keine Mühe, meinen Grauschimmel
führe ich selbst in den Stall, und binde ihn auch
selbst an, denn ich muß wissen wo er steht«
"Don't bother, I'll lead my gray horse into the stable myself,
and tie him up myself, for I must know where he stands;"

22.20 Dem Wirt kam das wunderlich vor und er meinte,
einer, der seinen Esel selbst besorgen müßte, hätte
nicht viel zu verzehren:
This seemed strange to the innkeeper, and he thought that
one who had to take care of his donkey himself would not
have much to eat:

22.21 als aber der Fremde in die Tasche griff, zwei
Goldstücke herausholte und sagte, er sollte nur etwas
Gutes für ihn einkaufen, so machte er große Augen,
lief und suchte das beste, das er auftreiben konnte.
But when the stranger reached into his pocket, took
out two pieces of gold and said that he should only buy
something good for him, he was wide-eyed, ran and looked
for the best he could find.

22.22 Nach der Mahlzeit fragte der Gast, was er schuldig
wäre, der Wirt wollte die doppelte Kreide nicht
sparen und sagte, noch ein paar Goldstücke müßte er
zulegen.
After the meal, the guest asked what he owed, the
innkeeper did not want to spare the double chalk and
said he would have to add a few more gold pieces.

22.23 Der Geselle griff in die Tasche,
The journeyman reached into his pocket,

22.24 aber sein Gold war eben zu Ende. »Wartet einen
Augenblick,
but his gold had just run out. "Wait a moment,

Herr Wirt.« sprach er, »ich will nur gehen und Gold
holen.«

22.25

innkeeper." he said, "I just want to go and get some gold."

nahm aber das Tischtuch mit.

22.26

But he took the tablecloth with him.

Der Wirt wußte nicht was das heißen sollte, war
neugierig, schlich ihm nach, und da der Gast die
Stallthür zuriegelte, so guckte er durch ein Astloch.

22.27

The innkeeper didn't know what that meant, was curious,
sneaked after him, and as the guest locked the stable door,
he peeked through a hole in the branch.

Der Fremde breitete unter dem Esel das Tuch aus,
rief,

22.28

The stranger spread the cloth under the donkey, called out,

»Bricklebrit.«

22.29

"Bricklebrit."

und augenblicklich fing das Tier an Gold zu speien
von hinten und vorn,

22.30

and immediately the animal began to spit gold from behind
and in front,

daß es ordentlich auf die Erde herabregnete.

22.31

so that it rained down on the ground.

»Ei der Tausend.« sagte der Wirt,

22.32

"A thousand eggs." said the innkeeper,

»da sind die Dukaten bald geprägt;

22.33

"the ducats will soon be minted;

so ein Geldbeutel ist nicht übel!«

22.34

such a purse is not bad!"

22.35 **Der Gast bezahlte seine Zeche und legte sich schlafen, der Wirt aber schlich in der Nacht herab in den Stall, führte den Münzmeister weg und band einen anderen Esel an seine Stelle.**

The guest paid his bill and went to bed, but the innkeeper crept down to the stable during the night, led the mintmaster away and tied another donkey in his place.

22.36 **Den folgenden Morgen in der Frühe zog der Geselle mit seinem Esel ab und meinte, er hätte seinen Goldesel.**

Early the next morning, the journeyman left with his donkey, thinking he had his golden ass.

22.37 **Mittags kam er bei seinem Vater an, der sich freute, als er ihn wieder sah und ihn gern aufnahm.**

At noon he arrived at his father's house, who was delighted to see him again and gladly took him in.

22.38 **»Was ist aus dir geworden, mein Sohn?« fragte der Alte.**

"What have you become, my son?" asked the old man.

22.39 **»Ein Müller, lieber Vater.« antwortete er.**

"A miller, dear father." he replied.

22.40 **»Was hast du von deiner Wanderschaft mitgebracht?«**

"What have you brought back from your wanderings?"

22.41 **»Weiter nichts als einen Esel.«**

"Nothing more than a donkey."

22.42 **»Esel giebt's hier genug.« sagte der Vater,**

"There are enough donkeys here." said the father,

»da wäre mir doch eine gute Ziege lieber gewesen.«   22.43
"I would have preferred a good goat."

»Ja.« antwortete der Sohn, »aber es ist kein gemeiner   22.44
Esel,
"Yes." answered the son, "but it is not a common donkey,

sondern ein Goldesel; wenn ich sage: »Bricklebrit.«   22.45
but a gold donkey; if I say, 'Bricklebrit.'

so speit Euch das gute Tier ein ganzes Tuch voll   22.46
Goldstücke.
the good animal will give you a whole cloth full of gold
pieces.

Laßt nur alle Verwandten herbeirufen,   22.47
Just send for all your relatives,

ich mache sie alle zu reichen Leuten.«   22.48
and I'll make them all rich."

»Das laß ich mir gefallen.« sagte der Schneider,   22.49
"I will put up with that." said the tailor,

»dann brauch ich mich mit der Nadel nicht weiter zu   22.50
quälen.«
"then I need not trouble myself further with the needle."

sprang selbst fort und rief die Verwandten herbei.   22.51
He sprang away himself and called the relatives.

Sobald sie beisammen waren, hieß sie der Müller   22.52
Platz machen, breitete sein Tuch aus und brachte den
Esel in die Stube.
As soon as they were together, the miller told them to make
room, spread out his cloth, and brought the donkey into
the parlor.

22.53 »Jetzt gebt acht.« sagte er und rief: »Bricklebrit.«

"Now take care." he said, and called out, "Bricklebrit."

22.54 aber es waren keine Goldstücke was herabfiel, und es zeigte sich, daß das Tier nichts von der Kunst verstand, denn es bringt's nicht jeder Esel so weit.

but there were no gold pieces that fell, and it was evident that the animal knew nothing of the art, for not every donkey gets so far.

22.55 Da machte der arme Müller ein langes Gesicht, sah, daß er betrogen war und bat die Verwandten um Verzeihung, die so arm heimgingen als sie gekommen waren.

Then the poor miller made a long face, saw that he had been cheated, and begged forgiveness of his relatives, who went home as poor as they had come.

22.56 Es blieb nichts übrig,

There was nothing left; the old man had to take up the needle again,

22.57 der Alte mußte wieder nach der Nadel greifen und der Junge sich bei einem Müller verdingen.

and the boy had to hire himself out to a miller.

23.1 Der dritte Bruder war zu einem Drechsler in die Lehre gegangen, und weil es ein kunstreiches Handwerk ist, mußte er am längsten lernen.

The third brother had been apprenticed to a turner, and because it is a skillful trade, he had to learn the longest.

23.2 Seine Brüder aber meldeten ihm in einem Briefe,

But his brothers wrote him a letter to tell him how badly they had fared,

wie schlimm es ihnen ergangen wäre und wie sie   23.3
der Wirt noch am letzten Abend um ihre schönen
Wünschdinge gebracht hätte.

and how the landlord had robbed them of their beautiful
things on the last evening.

Als der Drechsler nun ausgelernt hatte und wandern   23.4
sollte, so schenkte ihm sein Meister, weil er sich so
wohl gehalten, einen Sack und sagte:

When the woodturner had finished his apprenticeship and
was supposed to go on a journey, his master gave him a sack
because he had done so well and said:

»Es liegt ein Knüppel darin.« –   23.5

"There's a stick in it." –

»Den Sack kann ich umhängen und er kann mir gute   23.6
Dienste leisten,

"I can hang the sack around my neck and it can serve me
well,

aber was soll der Knüppel darin? der macht ihn nur   23.7
schwer.«

but what's with the club in it? It only makes it heavy."

»Das will ich dir sagen.« antwortete der Meister,   23.8

"I will tell you that." answered the master,

»hat dir jemand etwas zuleide gethan, so sprich nur,   23.9

"if any one has done you any harm, only say,

›Knüppel, aus dem Sack,‹   23.10

'Cudgel, out of the sack,'

23.11 so springt dir der Knüppel heraus unter die Leute und tanzt ihnen so lustig auf dem Rücken herum, daß sie sich acht Tage lang nicht regen und bewegen können und eher läßt er nicht ab, als bis du sagst,

and the cudgel will jump out among the people, and dance so merrily on their backs that they cannot move for eight days, and it will not let go till you say,

23.12 »Knüppel, in den Sack.«

'Cudgel, into the sack.«

23.13 Der Geselle dankte ihm, hing den Sack um und wenn ihm jemand zu nahe kam und auf den Leib wollte, so sprach er: »Knüppel, aus dem Sack.«

The journeyman thanked him, hung the sack round him, and if any one came too near and wanted to get at his body, he said, "Cudgel, out of the sack."

23.14 alsbald sprang der Knüppel heraus und klopfte einem nach dem anderen den Rock oder Wams gleich auf dem Rücken aus und wartete nicht erst, bis er ihn ausgezogen hatte, und das ging so geschwind, daß, ehe sich's einer versah, die Reihe schon an ihm war.

Immediately the cudgel sprang out, and knocked off the coat or doublet of one after another on his back, and did not wait till he had taken it off, and this was done so quickly that, before any one knew it, the turn was already upon him.

23.15 Der junge Drechsler langte zur Abendzeit in dem Wirtshaus an, wo seine Brüder waren betrogen worden.

The young turner arrived in the evening at the inn where his brothers had been cheated.

Er legte seinen Ranzen vor sich auf den Tisch und   23.16
fing an zu erzählen, was er alles Merkwürdiges in der
Welt gesehen habe.

He put his satchel on the table in front of him and began to
talk about all the strange things he had seen in the world.

»Ja.« sagte er,   23.17

"Yes." he said,

»man findet wohl ein Tischchen deck dich,   23.18

"you might find a table set for you,

einen Goldesel und dergleichen: 23.19

a golden donkey and the like:

lauter gute Dinge, die ich nicht verachte, aber das ist   23.20
alles nichts gegen den Schatz, den ich mir erworben
habe und mit mir da in meinem Sack führe.«

all good things that I don't despise, but all that is nothing
compared to the treasure that I have acquired and carry
with me in my sack."

Der Wirt spitzte die Ohren: 23.21

The innkeeper pricked up his ears:

»Was in aller Welt mag das sein?« dachte er,   23.22

"What on earth could that be?" he thought,

»der Sack ist wohl mit lauter Edelsteinen angefüllt;   23.23

"the sack is probably filled with precious stones;

den sollte ich billig auch noch haben,   23.24

I should have that too,

denn aller guten Dinge sind drei.« Als Schlafenszeit   23.25
war,

for all good things come in threes." When bedtime came,

23.26 streckte sich der Gast auf die Bank und legte seinen
Sack als Kopfkissen unter.
the guest stretched out on the bench and put his sack under
his pillow.

23.27 Der Wirt, als er meinte, der Gast läge in tiefem
Schlaf, ging herbei, rückte und zog ganz sachte
und vorsichtig an dem Sack, ob er ihn vielleicht
wegziehen und einen anderen unterlegen könnte.
The innkeeper, thinking the guest was in a deep sleep, went
over, moved and pulled the sack very gently and carefully
to see if he could perhaps pull it away and put another one
underneath.

23.28 Der Drechsler aber hatte schon lange darauf
gewartet;
The turner, however, had been waiting a long time for this;

23.29 wie nun der Wirt einen herzhaften Ruck thun wollte,
rief er,
and as the innkeeper was about to give it a hearty jerk, he
called out,

23.30 »Knüppel, aus dem Sack.«
"Cudgel, out of the sack."

23.31 Alsbald fuhr das Knüppelchen heraus, dem Wirt
auf den Leib und rieb ihm die Nähte, daß es eine Art
hatte.
Immediately the little cudgel came out, struck the
innkeeper on the body, and rubbed his seams so hard
that it made a sort of a mess.

Der Wirt schrie zum Erbarmen, aber je lauter er
schrie, desto kräftiger schlug der Knüppel ihm den
Takt dazu auf dem Rücken, bis er endlich erschöpft
zur Erde fiel.   23.32

The innkeeper cried out for mercy, but the louder he cried,
the harder the cudgel beat his back, until at last he fell
exhausted to the ground.

Da sprach der Drechsler: 23.33

Then the turner said,

»Wenn du das Tischchen deck dich und den Goldesel
nicht wieder herausgiebst,   23.34

"If you don't give back the tablecloth and the gold donkey,

so soll der Tanz von neuem angehen.«   23.35

the dance will start again."

»Ach nein.«   23.36

"Oh no."

rief der Wirt ganz kleinlaut, ich gebe alles gern
wieder heraus, laßt nur den verwünschten Kobold
wieder in den Sack kriechen.«   23.37

cried the innkeeper meekly, "I will gladly give it all back,
just let the cursed leprechaun crawl back into the sack."

Da sprach der Geselle,   23.38

Then the journeyman said,

»Ich will Gnade für Recht ergehen lassen,   23.39

"I will give mercy for justice,

aber hüte dich vor Schaden!« dann rief er: »Knüppel,   23.40

but beware of harm!" Then he cried, "Cudgel,

23.41 in den Sack!« und ließ ihn ruhen.
into the sack!" and let him rest.

24.1 Der Drechsler zog am anderen Morgen mit dem Tischchen deck dich und dem Goldesel heim zu seinem Vater.
The next morning, the woodturner went home to his father with the table and the gold donkey.

24.2 Der Schneider freute sich, als er ihn wieder sah und fragte auch ihn, was er in der Fremde gelernt hätte.
The tailor was delighted when he saw him again and asked him what he had learned in a foreign country.

24.3 »Lieber Vater.« antwortete er,
"Dear father." he replied,

24.4 »ich bin ein Drechsler geworden.«
"I have become a wood turner."

24.5 »Ein kunstreiches Handwerk.« sagte der Vater,
"A skillful craft." said his father,

24.6 was hast du von der Wanderschaft mitgebracht?«
"what have you brought back from your travels?"

24.7 »Ein kostbares Stück, lieber Vater.« antwortete der Sohn,
"A precious piece, dear father." replied the son,

24.8 »einen Knüppel in dem Sack.«
"a club in the sack."

24.9 »Was!« rief der Vater, »einen Knüppel!
"What!" cried the father, "a club!

das ist der Mühe wert!   24.10

that's worth the trouble!

den kannst du dir von jedem Baume abhauen.«   24.11

you can cut it from any tree."

»Aber Vater, sage ich: ›Knüppel, aus dem Sack,‹   24.12

"But, father, if I say, 'Cudgel, out of the sack,'

so springt der Knüppel heraus und macht mit dem,   24.13
der es nicht gut mit mir meint, einen schlimmen
Tanz und läßt nicht eher nach, als bis er auf der Erde
liegt und um gut Wetter bittet.

the cudgel will jump out and do a bad dance with him who
does not mean me well, and will not let up until he lies on
the ground and begs for good weather.

Seht Ihr, mit diesem Knüppel habe ich das Tischchen   24.14
deck dich und den Goldesel wieder herbeigeschafft,
die der diebische Wirt meinen Brüdern abgenommen
hatte.

You see, with this cudgel I have brought back the table and
the golden ass, which the thieving innkeeper had taken
from my brothers.

Jetzt laßt sie beide rufen und ladet alle Verwandten   24.15
ein,

Now let them both be summoned and invite all their
relatives,

ich will sie speisen und tränken und will ihnen die   24.16
Taschen noch mit Gold füllen.«

I will feed and water them and fill their pockets with gold."

Der alte Schneider wollte nicht recht trauen,   24.17

The old tailor did not really want to trust them,

24.18 **brachte aber doch die Verwandten zusammen.**
but he brought the relatives together.

24.19 **Da deckte der Drechsler ein Tuch in die Stube,**
Then the turner laid a cloth in the parlor,

24.20 **führte den Goldesel herein und sagte zu seinem Bruder:**
brought in the gold donkey and said to his brother:

24.21 **»Nun, lieber Bruder, sprich mit ihm.« Der Müller sagte,**
"Now, dear brother, talk to him." The miller said,

24.22 **»Bricklebrit.«**
"Bricklebrit."

24.23 **und augenblicklich sprangen die Goldstücke auf das Tuch herab als käme ein Platzregen, und der Esel hörte nicht eher auf, als bis alle soviel hatten, daß sie nicht mehr tragen konnten.**
and instantly the gold pieces sprang down on the cloth as if it were a downpour, and the donkey did not stop until they all had so much that they could carry no more.

24.24 **(Ich sehe dir's an, du wärst auch gern dabei gewesen.)**
(I can see that you would have liked to have been there too.)

24.25 **Dann holte der Drechsler das Tischchen und sagte,**
Then the carpenter fetched the little table and said,

24.26 **»Lieber Bruder, nun sprich mit ihm.«**
"Dear brother, now talk to him."

24.27 **Und kaum hatte der Schreiner »Tischchen, deck dich«**
And no sooner had the carpenter said, "Set the table,"

gesagt, so war es gedeckt und mit den schönsten
Schüsseln reichlich besetzt.
24.28

than it was laid and lavishly set with the most beautiful
dishes.

Da ward eine Mahlzeit gehalten, wie der gute
Schneider noch keine in seinem Hause erlebt hatte
und die ganze Verwandtschaft blieb beisammen bis in
die Nacht und waren alle lustig und vergnügt.
24.29

Then they had a meal such as the good tailor had never
seen in his house, and the whole family stayed together till
nightfall, and were all merry and happy.

Der Schneider verschloß Nadel und Zwirn, Elle und
Bügeleisen in einen Schrank und lebte mit seinen
drei Söhnen in Freude und Herrlichkeit,
24.30

The tailor locked up his needle and twine, his ell and iron in
a cupboard, and lived with his three sons in joy and glory,

Wo ist aber die Ziege hingekommen, die schuld war,
daß der Schneider seine Söhne fortjagte?
25.1

But where did the goat go that was to blame for the tailor
chasing his sons away?

Das will ich dir sagen.
25.2

I will tell you.

Sie schämte sich, daß sie einen kahlen Kopf hatte, lief
in eine Fuchshöhle und verkroch sich hinein.
25.3

She was ashamed that she had a bald head, ran into a fox's
den and hid herself inside.

25.4 Als der Fuchs nach Hause kam, funkelten ihm ein paar große Augen aus der Dunkelheit entgegen, daß er erschrak und wieder zurücklief.

When the fox came home, a pair of large eyes sparkled at him from the darkness, so that he was frightened and ran back again.

25.5 Der Bär begegnete ihm und da der Fuchs ganz verstört aussah, so sprach er:

The bear met him, and as the fox looked quite disturbed, he said,

25.6 »Was ist dir, Bruder Fuchs, was machst du für ein Gesicht?«

"What is the matter with you, brother fox, what kind of face are you making?"

25.7 »Ach.« antwortete der Rote,

"Oh." replied the red bear,

25.8 »ein grimmiges Tier sitzt in meiner Höhle und hat mich mit feurigen Augen angeglotzt.«

"a fierce animal is sitting in my cave and has been staring at me with fiery eyes."

25.9 »Das wollen wir bald austreiben.«

"We will soon drive it out."

25.10 sprach der Bär, ging mit zur Höhle und schaute hinein: als er aber die feurigen Augen erblickte, wandelte ihn ebenfalls Furcht an; er wollte mit dem grimmigen Tiere nichts zu thun haben und nahm Reißaus.

said the bear, and went along to the cave and looked in; but when he saw the fiery eyes, he also became afraid; he did not want to have anything to do with the fierce beast and ran away.

Die Biene begegnete ihm und da sie merkte, daß es
ihm in seiner Haut nicht wohl zu Mute war, sprach
sie:

25.11

The bee met him, and perceiving that he was not
comfortable in his own skin, she said,

»Bär, du machst ja ein gewaltig verdrießlich Gesicht,
wo ist deine Lustigkeit geblieben?«

25.12

"Bear, you make a very peevish face; where is your mirth?"

»Du hast gut reden.«

25.13

"You speak well."

antwortete der Bär, es sitzt ein grimmiges Tier mit
Glotzaugen in dem Hause des Roten und wir können
es nicht herausjagen.«

25.14

answered the bear, "there is a fierce beast with goggle eyes
in the red man's house, and we can't chase it out."

Die Biene sprach:

25.15

The bee said,

»Du dauerst mich, Bär, ich bin ein armes schwaches,
Geschöpf, das ihr im Wege nicht anguckt, aber ich
glaube doch, daß ich euch helfen kann.«

25.16

"You keep me, bear, I am a poor weak creature that you do
not look at in the way, but I believe I can help you."

Sie flog in die Fuchshöhle, setzte sich der Ziege
auf den glatten geschorenen Kopf und stach sie so
gewaltig, daß sie aufsprang

25.17

She flew into the fox's den, sat down on the goat's smooth,
shaven head, and stung it so violently that it jumped up,
cried

»meh! meh!« schrie und wie toll in die Welt
hineinlief,

25.18

"meh! meh!" and ran off like mad into the world,

25.19 **und weiß niemand auf diese Stunde wo sie hingelaufen ist.**

and no one knows at this hour where it ran off to.

König Drosselbart

King Thrushbeard

1.1 Ein König hatte eine Tochter, die war über alle
Maßen schön aber dabei so stolz und übermütig,
daß ihr kein Freier gut genug war.

A king had a daughter who was beautiful beyond measure
but so proud and cocky that no suitor was good enough for
her.

1.2 Sie wies einen nach dem anderen ab, und trieb noch
dazu Spott mit ihnen.

She rejected one after the other and made fun of them.

1.3 Einmal ließ der König ein großes Fest anstellen
und ladete dazu aus der Nähe und Ferne die
heiratslustigen Männer ein.

Once the king ordered a great feast and invited marriage-
minded men from near and far.

1.4 Sie wurden alle in eine Reihe nach Rang und Stand
geordnet;

They were all lined up according to rank and status;

erst kamen die Könige, dann die Herzöge, die
Fürsten, Grafen und Freiherrn, zuletzt die Edelleute. 1.5
first came the kings, then the dukes, princes, counts and
barons, and finally the noblemen.

Nun ward die Königstochter durch die Reihen
geführt, 1.6
Now the king's daughter was led through the ranks,

aber an jedem hatte sie etwas auszusetzen. 1.7
but she found fault with each one.

Der eine war ihr zu dick, »das Weinfaß!« sprach sie. 1.8
One was too fat for her, "the wine barrel!" she said.

Der andere zu lang, »lang und schwank hat keinen
Gang.« 1.9
The other was too long, "long and swaying has no gait."

Der dritte zu kurz, »kurz und dick hat kein Geschick.« 1.10
The third was too short, "short and fat has no skill."

Der vierte zu blaß, »der bleiche Tod!« 1.11
The fourth was too pale, "the pale death!"

der fünfte zu rot, »der Zinshahn!« 1.12
the fifth too red, "the interest cock!"

der sechste war nicht gerad genug, »grünes Holz, 1.13
the sixth was not straight enough, "green wood,

hinterm Ofen getrocknet!« 1.14
dried behind the stove!"

1.15 Und so hatte sie an einem jeden etwas auszusetzen, besonders aber machte sie sich über einen guten König lustig, der ganz oben stand, und dem das Kinn ein wenig krumm gewachsen war.

And so she found fault with every one of them, but she especially made fun of a good king who stood at the very top and whose chin had grown a little crooked.

1.16 »Ei.« rief sie und lachte,

"Egg." she cried, laughing,

1.17 »der hat ein Kinn wie die Drossel einen Schnabel.«

"he has a chin like a thrush has a beak."

1.18 und seit der Zeit bekam er den Namen Drosselbart.

and from that time he was called Thrushbeard.

1.19 Der alte König aber, als er sah, daß seine Tochter nichts that als über die Leute spotten, und alle Freier, die da versammelt waren, verschmähte, ward er zornig und schwur, sie sollte den ersten besten Bettler zum Manne nehmen, der vor seine Thür käme.

But the old king, when he saw that his daughter did nothing but mock at the people, and spurned all the suitors who were assembled there, became angry, and swore that she should take the first best beggar to husband who came to his door.

2.1 Ein paar Tage darauf hub ein Spielmann an unter dem Fenster zu singen,

A few days later,

2.2 um damit ein geringes Almosen zu verdienen.

a minstrel began to sing under the window to earn a small alms.

Als es der König hörte, sprach er: »Laßt ihn   2.3
heraufkommen.«
When the king heard it, he said, "Let him come up."

Da trat der Spielmann in seinen schmutzigen   2.4
verlumpten Kleidern herein, sang vor dem König
und seiner Tochter und bat, als er fertig war, um eine
milde Gabe.
Then the minstrel entered in his dirty, ragged clothes,
sang before the King and his daughter, and when he had
finished, asked for a pittance.

Der König sprach: 2.5
The king said,

»Dein Gesang hat mir so wohl gefallen, daß ich dir   2.6
meine Tochter da zur Frau geben will.«
"Your singing has pleased me so much that I will give you
my daughter as your wife."

Die Königstochter erschrak, aber der König sagte: 2.7
The king's daughter was frightened, but the king said,

»Ich habe den Eid gethan, dich dem ersten besten   2.8
Bettelmann zu geben, den will ich auch halten.«
"I have taken an oath to give you to the first best beggar,
and I will keep it."

Es half keine Einrede, der Pfarrer ward geholt, und   2.9
sie mußte sich gleich mit dem Spielmann trauen
lassen.
There was no help for it, the priest was sent for, and she had
to be married to the minstrel at once.

Als das geschehen war, sprach der König: 2.10
When this was done, the king said,

2.11 »Nun schickt sich's nicht, daß du als ein Bettelweib
noch länger in meinem Schloß bleibst, du kannst nur
mit deinem Manne fortziehen.«

"Now it is not fit that you should remain any longer in my
castle as a beggar woman; you can only go away with your
husband."

3.1 Der Bettelmann führte sie an der Hand hinaus und
sie mußte mit ihm zu Fuß fortgehen.

The beggar led her out by the hand and she had to walk
away with him.

3.2 Als sie in einen großen Wald kamen, da fragte sie:

When they came to a large forest, she asked:

»Ach, wem gehört der
schöne Wald?«

"Oh, who owns the
beautiful forest?"

»Der gehört dem König
Drosselbart;

"It belongs to King
Thrushbeard;

hättst du'n genommen, so
wär er dein.«

If you had taken it, it
would have been yours."

»Ich arme Jungfer zart,

"I poor maiden tender,

ach, hätt ich genommen
den König Drosselbart!«

oh, if I had taken King
Thrushbeard!"

5.1 Darauf kamen sie über eine Wiese, da fragte sie
wieder

Then they came across a meadow and she asked again

»Wem gehört die schöne
grüne Wiese?«

"Who owns the beautiful
green meadow?"

»Sie gehört dem König Drosselbart;

"It belongs to King Thrushbeard;

hättst du'n genommen, so wär sie dein.«

If you had taken it, it would have been yours."

»Ich arme Jungfer zart,

"I poor maiden tender,

ach, hätt ich genommen den König Drosselbart!«

oh, if I had taken King Thrushbeard!"

Dann kamen sie durch eine große Stadt, da fragte sie wieder: 7.1

Then they passed through a large town and she asked again:

»Wem gehört diese schöne große Stadt?«

"Who owns this beautiful big city?"

»Sie gehört dem König Drosselbart;

"It belongs to King Thrushbeard;

hättst du'n genommen, so wär sie dein.«

If you had taken it, it would have been yours."

»Ich arme Jungfer zart,

"I poor maiden tender,

ach, hätt ich genommen den König Drosselbart!«

oh, if I had taken King Thrushbeard!"

»Es gefällt mir gar nicht.« sprach der Spielmann,   9.1

"I don't like it at all." said the minstrel,

»daß du dir immer einen anderen zum Mann wünschest: 9.2

"that you always want someone else for a husband:

9.3 bin ich dir nicht gut genug?«
am I not good enough for you?"

9.4 Endlich kamen sie an ein ganz kleines Häuschen, da sprach sie:
At last they came to a very small cottage, and there she said:

»Ach, Gott, was ist das Haus so klein!	"Oh, God, this house is so small!
wem mag das elende winzige Häuschen sein?«	Who might this miserable tiny house be for?"

11.1 Der Spielmann antwortete: »Das ist mein und dein Haus,
The minstrel replied, "This is my house and yours,

11.2 wo wir zusammen wohnen.«
where we live together."

11.3 Sie mußte sich bücken, damit sie zu der niedrigen Thür hineinkam.
She had to stoop to get in at the low door.

11.4 »Wo sind die Diener?« sprach die Königstochter.
"Where are the servants?" said the king's daughter.

11.5 »Was Diener!« antwortete der Bettelmann,
"What servants!" answered the mendicant,

11.6 »du mußt selber thun, was du willst gethan haben.
"you must do yourself what you want done.

Mach nur gleich Feuer an und stell Wasser auf, daß   11.7
du mir mein Essen kochst;

Only light a fire at once, and put on some water, that you
may cook my dinner;

ich bin ganz müde.«   11.8

I am quite tired."

Die Königstochter verstand aber nichts vom   11.9
Feueranmachen und Kochen, und der Bettelmann
mußte selber mit Hand anlegen, daß es noch so
leidlich ging.

But the king's daughter knew nothing about lighting a fire
and cooking, and the beggar had to help himself to make it
work.

Als sie die schmale Kost verzehrt hatten, legten sie   11.10
sich zu Bett; aber am Morgen trieb er sie schon ganz
früh heraus, weil sie das Haus besorgen sollte.

When they had eaten their scanty fare, they went to bed,
but in the morning he drove her out very early, because she
was to take care of the house.

Ein Paar Tage lebten sie auf diese Art schlecht und   11.11
recht und zehrten ihren Vorrat auf.

They lived like this for a couple of days and used up their
food.

Da sprach der Mann: 11.12

Then the man said,

»Frau, so geht's nicht länger, daß wir hier zehren und   11.13
nichts verdienen.

"Wife, we can't go on living here and earning nothing.

Du sollst Körbe flechten.« Er ging aus,   11.14

You shall weave baskets." He went out,

11.15 schnitt Weiden und brachte sie heim;
cut willows and brought them home;

11.16 da fing sie an zu flechten,
then she began to weave,

11.17 aber die harten Weiden stachen ihr die zarten Hände wund.
but the hard willows pricked her tender hands.

11.18 »Ich sehe, das geht nicht.« sprach der Mann,
"I see you can't do that." said the man,

11.19 »spinn lieber, vielleicht kannst du das besser.«
"you had better spin, perhaps you can do it better."

11.20 Sie setzte sich hin und versuchte zu spinnen, aber der harte Faden schnitt ihr bald in die weichen Finger, daß das Blut daran herunterlief.
She sat down and tried to spin, but the hard thread soon cut her soft fingers so that the blood ran down them.

11.21 »Siehst du.« sprach der Mann,
"You see." said the man,

11.22 »du taugst zu keiner Arbeit,
"you're no good for any work,

11.23 mit dir bin ich schlimm angekommen.
I've come to a bad end with you.

11.24 Nun will ich's versuchen und einen Handel mit Töpfen und irdenem Geschirr anfangen;
Now I will try it, and begin a trade in pots and earthenware;

du sollst dich auf den Markt setzen und die Ware feilhalten.«

11.25

you shall sit down in the market and hawk the goods."

»Ach.« dachte sie,

11.26

"Oh." she thought,

»wenn auf den Markt Leute aus meines Vaters Reich kommen, und sehen mich da sitzen und feilhalten, wie werden sie mich verspotten!«

11.27

"if people from my father's kingdom come to the market and see me sitting there and haggling, how they will mock me!"

Aber es half nichts, sie mußte sich fügen, wenn sie nicht Hungers sterben wollten.

11.28

But it was no use, she had to submit if they were not to die of hunger.

Das erste Mal ging's gut, denn die Leute kauften der Frau, weil sie schön war, gern ihre Ware ab und bezahlten was sie forderte;

11.29

The first time it went well, for the people gladly bought the woman's goods because she was beautiful, and paid what she asked;

ja,

11.30

indeed,

viele gaben ihr das Geld und ließen ihr die Töpfe noch dazu.

11.31

many gave her the money and left her the pots as well.

Nun lebten sie von dem Erworbenen, so lange es dauerte, da handelte der Mann wieder eine Menge neues Geschirr ein.

11.32

Now they lived on what they had bought for as long as it took, when the man bought another lot of new crockery.

11.33 Sie setzte sich damit an eine Ecke des Marktes und stellte es um sich her und hielt feil.
She sat down at a corner of the market and placed it around her, offering it for sale.

11.34 Da kam plötzlich ein trunkener Husar dahergejagt und ritt geradezu in die Töpfe hinein,
Then suddenly a drunken hussar came chasing along and rode straight into the pots,

11.35 daß alles in tausend Scherben zersprang.
shattering everything into a thousand pieces.

11.36 Sie fing an zu weinen und wußte vor Angst nicht was sie anfangen sollte.
She began to weep and was frightened and did not know what to do.

11.37 »Ach, wie wird mir's ergehen!« rief sie,
"Oh, what will happen to me!" she cried,

11.38 »was wird mein Mann dazu sagen!«
"what will my husband say!"

11.39 Sie lief heim und erzählte ihm das Unglück.
She ran home and told him about her misfortune.

11.40 »Wer setzt sich auch an die Ecke des Marktes mit irdenem Geschirr!«
"Who sits down at the corner of the market with earthenware dishes!"

11.41 sprach der Mann,
said the man,

11.42 »laß nur das Weinen, ich sehe wohl, du bist zu keiner ordentlichen Arbeit zu gebrauchen.
"stop crying, I see you are not fit for any proper work.

Da bin ich in unseres Königs Schloß gewesen und habe gefragt, ob sie nicht eine Küchenmagd brauchen könnten, und sie haben mir versprochen, sie wollten dich dazu nehmen; 11.43

So I went to our King's castle and asked if they couldn't use a kitchen maid, and they promised me they would take you on;

dafür bekommst du freies Essen.« 11.44

in return you would get free food."

Nun ward die Königstochter eine Küchenmagd, 12.1

Now the king's daughter became a kitchen maid,

mußte dem Koch zur Hand gehen und die sauerste Arbeit thun. 12.2

and had to help the cook and do the sourest work.

Sie machte sich in beiden Taschen ein Töpfchen fest, darin brachte sie nach Haus, was ihr von dem Übriggebliebenen zu teil ward und davon nährten sie sich. 12.3

She made herself a little pot in both her pockets, in which she brought home what was left to her, and from this they fed.

Es trug sich zu, daß die Hochzeit des ältesten Königssohnes sollte gefeiert werden, da ging die arme Frau hinauf, stellte sich vor die Saalthür und wollte zusehen. 12.4

It came to pass that the wedding of the eldest son of the King was to be celebrated, and the poor woman went up, stood at the door of the hall, and wished to look on.

12.5 Als nun die Lichter angezündet waren und immer einer schöner als der andere hereintrat, und alles voll Pracht und Herrlichkeit war, da dachte sie mit betrübtem Herzen an ihr Schicksal und verwünschte ihren Stolz und Übermut, der sie erniedrigt und in so große Armut gestürzt hatte.

When the lights were lighted, and each one came in more beautiful than the other, and everything was full of splendor and magnificence, she thought with a sad heart of her fate, and cursed her pride and arrogance, which had degraded her and plunged her into such great poverty.

12.6 Von den köstlichen Speisen, die da ein - und ausgetragen wurden, und von welchen der Geruch zu ihr aufstieg, warfen ihr Diener manchmal ein paar Brocken zu, die that sie in ihr Töpfchen und wollte es heimtragen.

Sometimes servants would throw her a few pieces of the delicious food that was brought in and taken out, and she would put them in her little pot and carry them home.

12.7 Auf einmal trat der Königssohn herein, war in Sammet und Seide gekleidet und hatte goldene Ketten um den Hals.

Suddenly the king's son came in, dressed in velvet and silk, with golden chains around his neck.

12.8 Und als er die schöne Frau in der Thür stehen sah, ergriff er sie bei der Hand und wollte mit ihr tanzen, aber sie weigerte sich und erschrak, denn sie sah, daß es der König Drosselbart war, der um sie gefreit und den sie mit Spott abgewiesen hatte.

And when he saw the beautiful woman standing in the doorway, he seized her by the hand and wanted to dance with her, but she refused and was frightened, for she saw that it was King Thrushbeard who had courted her and whom she had rejected with mockery.

Ihr Sträuben half nichts, er zog sie in den Saal; da 12.9
zerriß das Band, an welchem die Taschen hingen und
die Töpfe fielen heraus, daß die Suppe floß und die
Brocken umhersprangen.

Her refusal was of no avail, he drew her into the hall, and
the ribbon on which the bags were hanging was torn, and
the pots fell out, so that the soup flowed and the lumps flew
about.

Und wie das die Leute sahen, entstand ein 12.10
allgemeines Gelächter und Spotten und sie war so
beschämt, daß sie sich lieber tausend Klafter unter
die Erde gewünscht hätte.

And when the people saw this, there was a general laugh
and mockery, and she was so ashamed that she would
rather have wished herself a thousand fathoms under the
ground.

Sie sprang zur Thür hinaus und sollte entfliehen, aber 12.11
auf der Treppe holte sie ein Mann ein und brachte
sie zurück; und wie sie ihn ansah, war es wieder der
König Drosselbart.

She jumped out of the door and was about to escape, but
a man caught her on the stairs and brought her back, and
when she looked at him it was King Thrushbeard again.

Er sprach ihr freundlich zu: 12.12

He said to her kindly,

»Fürchte dich nicht, ich und der Spielmann, der mit 12.13
dir in dem elenden Häuschen gewohnt hat, sind eins;

"Fear not, I and the minstrel who lived with you in the
miserable little house are one;

12.14 dir zuliebe habe ich mich so verstellt, und der Husar, der dir die Töpfe entzwei geritten hat, bin ich auch gewesen.
I have disguised myself thus for your sake, and I was also the hussar who broke your pots.

12.15 Das alles ist geschehen,
All this has been done to bend your proud spirit and to punish you for your arrogance,

12.16 um deinen stolzen Sinn zu beugen und dich für deinen Hochmut zu strafen; womit du mich verspottet hast.«
with which you have mocked me."

12.17 Da weinte sie bitterlich und sagte:
Then she wept bitterly and said,

12.18 »Ich habe großes Unrecht gehabt und bin nicht wert deine Frau zu sein.«
"I have been greatly wronged and am not worthy to be your wife."

12.19 Er aber sprach:
But he said:

12.20 »Tröste dich, die bösen Tage sind vorüber, jetzt wollen wir unsere Hochzeit feiern.«
"Take comfort, the bad days are over, now we want to celebrate our wedding."

Da kamen die Kammerfrauen und thaten ihr die 12.21
prächtigsten Kleider an und ihr Vater kam und
der ganze Hof, und wünschten ihr Glück zu ihrer
Vermählung mit dem König Drosselbart, und die
rechte Freude fing jetzt erst an.

Then the ladies-in-waiting came and dressed her in the
most splendid clothes, and her father and the whole court
came and wished her happiness on her marriage to King
Thrushbeard, and the real joy only now began.

Ich wollte, du und ich, wir wären auch dabei 12.22
gewesen.

I wish you and I had been there too.

Die kluge Bauerntochter

The Clever Farmer's Daughter

1.1 Es war einmal ein armer Bauer, der hatte kein Land, nur ein kleines Häuschen und eine alleinige Tochter.
Once upon a time there was a poor farmer who had no land, just a small house and an only daughter.

1.2 Da sprach die Tochter:
So the daughter said:

1.3 »Wir sollten den Herrn König um ein Stückchen Rottland bitten.«
"We should ask the king for a piece of red land."

1.4 Da der König ihre Armut hörte, schenkte er ihnen auch ein Eckchen Rasen, den hackte sie und ihr Vater um, und wollte ein wenig Korn und derartige Frucht drauf säen.
When the king heard of their poverty, he also gave them a corner of grass, which she and her father chopped up and wanted to sow a little grain and fruit on it.

1.5 Als sie den Acker beinahe herum hatten,
When they had nearly finished the field,

so fanden sie in der Erde einen Mörser von purem Gold.

1.6

they found a mortar of pure gold in the ground.

»Hör.« sagt der Vater zu dem Mädchen,

1.7

"Listen." said the father to the girl,

»weil unser Herr König ist so gnädig gewesen, und hat uns diesen Acker geschenkt, so müssen wir ihm den Mörser dafür geben.«

1.8

"because our lord king has been so gracious and has given us this field, we must give him the mortar for it."

Die Tochter aber wollte es nicht bewilligen und sagte:

1.9

But the daughter would not allow it and said,

»Vater, wenn wir den Mörser haben und haben den Stößer nicht, dann müssen wir auch den Stößer herbeischaffen, darum schweigt lieber still.«

1.10

"Father, if we have the mortar and don't have the pestle, then we must also get the pestle, so you'd better keep quiet."

Er wollte ihr aber nicht gehorchen, nahm den Mörser, trug ihn zum Herrn König, und sagte, den hätte er gefunden in der Heide, ob er ihn als eine Verehrung annehmen wollte.

1.11

But he would not obey her, took the mortar, carried it to the king, and said that he had found it on the heath, and would he accept it as a gift.

Der König nahm den Mörser und fragte, ob er nichts mehr gefunden hätte?

1.12

The king took the mortar and asked if he had found nothing more?

»Nein.« antwortete der Bauer.

1.13

"No." replied the farmer.

1.14 Da sagte der König er sollte nun auch den Stößer herbeischaffen.

Then the king told him to bring the pestle as well.

1.15 Der Bauer sprach,

The farmer said that they had not found it,

1.16 den hätten sie nicht gefunden;

but that helped him as much as if he had said it to the wind;

1.17 aber das half ihm so viel, als hätte er's in den Wind gesagt, er ward ins Gefängnis gesetzt, und sollte so lange da sitzen, bis er den Stößer herbeigeschafft hätte.

he was put in prison and was to sit there until he had brought the pestle.

1.18 Die Bedienten mußten ihm täglich Wasser und Brot bringen, was man so in dem Gefängnis kriegt, da hörten sie, wie der Mann fortwährend schrie: »Ach, hätt' ich meiner Tochter gehört!

The servants had to bring him bread and water every day, which is what you get in prison, when they heard the man crying out continually, "Oh, if I had listened to my daughter!

1.19 ach, ach, hätt ich meiner Tochter gehört!«

oh, oh, if I had listened to my daughter!"

1.20 Da gingen die Bedienten, zum König und sprachen das, wie der Gefangene fortwährend schrie: »Ach, hätt' ich doch meiner Tochter gehört!«

Then the servants went to the king and told him how the prisoner kept crying out, "Oh, if only I had listened to my daughter!"

1.21 und wollte nicht essen und nicht trinken.

and would not eat or drink.

Da befahl er den Bedienten, sie sollten den   1.22
Gefangenen vor ihn bringen, und da fragte ihn der
Herr König, warum er fortwährend schrie: »Ach,
hätt' ich meiner Tochter gehört!

Then he ordered the servants to bring the prisoner before
him, and the king asked him why he kept crying out, "Oh, if
I had only listened to my daughter!

Was hat Eure Tochter denn gesagt?«   1.23

What did your daughter say?"

»Ja, sie hat gesprochen, ich sollte den Mörser nicht   1.24
bringen, sonst müßt ich auch den Stößer schaffen.«

"Yes, she said that I should not bring the mortar, otherwise
I would have to bring the pestle as well."

»Habt Ihr so eine kluge Tochter, so laßt sie einmal   1.25
herkommen.«

"If you have such a clever daughter, let her come here
once."

Also mußte sie vor den König kommen, der fragte sie,   1.26
ob sie denn so klug wäre, und sagte, er wolle ihr ein
Rätsel aufgeben, wenn sie das treffen könnte, dann
wollte er sie heiraten.

So she had to come before the King, who asked her if she
was so clever, and said he wanted to give her a riddle, and if
she could solve it, he would marry her.

Da sprach sie gleich ja, sie wollt's erraten.   1.27

She immediately said yes, she wanted to guess it.

Da sagte der König: 1.28

Then the king said,

1.29 »Komm zu mir, nicht gekleidet, nicht nackend, nicht geritten, nicht gefahren, nicht in dem Weg, nicht außer dem Weg, und wenn du das kannst, will ich dich heiraten.«

"Come to me, not clothed, not naked, not riding, not driving, not in the way, not out of the way, and if you can do that, I will marry you."

1.30 Da ging sie hin und zog sich aus splitternackend, da war sie nicht gekleidet, und nahm ein großes Fischgarn, und setzte sich hinein und wickelte es ganz um sich herum, da war sie nicht nackend;

So she went and undressed herself stark naked, for she was not clothed, and took a large fish-rope, and sat in it, and wrapped it all round her, for she was not naked;

1.31 und borgte einen Esel fürs Geld und band dem Esel das Fischgarn an den Schwanz, darin er sie fortschleppen mußte, und war das nicht geritten und nicht gefahren;

And she borrowed an ass for money, and tied the fish-thread to the ass's tail, in which he had to drag her away, and he did not ride or drive her;

1.32 der Esel mußte sie aber in dem Fahrgleise schleppen, sodaß sie nur mit der großen Zehe auf die Erde kam, und war das nicht in dem Wege und nicht außer dem Wege.

but the ass had to drag her in the track, so that she only got her big toe on the ground, and she was not in the way and not out of the way.

1.33 Und wie sie so daher kam, sagte der König, sie hätte das Rätsel getroffen und es wäre alles erfüllt.

And as she came along thus, the king said she had met the riddle, and all was accomplished.

Da ließ er ihren Vater los aus dem Gefängnis und nahm sie zu sich als seine Gemahlin und befahl ihr das ganze königliche Gut an.

1.34

So he released her father from prison and took her to himself as his wife and gave her the entire royal estate.

Nun waren etliche Jahre herum; als der Herr König einmal auf die Parade zog, da trug es sich zu, daß Bauern mit ihren Wagen vor dem Schloß hielten, die hatten Holz verkauft; etliche hatten Ochsen vorgespannt und etliche Pferde.

2.1

Now some years had passed, and once when the King was going on parade, it happened that some peasants were stopping in front of the castle with their carts, and they were selling wood; some of them had oxen harnessed to them, and several horses.

Da war ein Bauer, der hatte drei Pferde, davon kriegte eins ein junges Füllchen, das lief weg und legte sich mitten zwischen zwei Ochsen, die vor dem Wagen waren.

2.2

There was a farmer who had three horses, one of which got a young filly, which ran away and lay down in the middle between two oxen that were in front of the cart.

Als nun die Bauern zusammenkamen, fingen sie an sich zu zanken, zu schmeißen und zu lärmen, und der Ochsenbauer wollte das Füllchen behalten und sagte, die Ochsen hätten's gehabt, und der andere sagte nein, seine Pferde hätten's gehabt, und es wäre sein.

2.3

Now when the farmers came together, they began to quarrel, to throw and to make a noise, and the ox farmer wanted to keep the little filling and said that the oxen had had it, and the other said no, his horses had had it, and it was his.

2.4 Der Zank kam vor den König, und er that den
Ausspruch: wo das Füllen gelegen hätte, da sollt es
bleiben;

The quarrel came before the king, and he said that where
the stuffing had been, there it should remain;

2.5 und also bekam's der Ochsenbauer, dem's doch nicht
gehörte.

and so the ox-man got it, to whom it did not belong.

2.6 Da ging der andere weg,

Then the other went away,

2.7 weinte und lamentierte über sein Füllchen.

weeping and lamenting over his little cornucopia.

2.8 Nun hatte er gehört, daß die Frau Königin so
gnädig wäre, weil sie auch von armen Bauersleuten
gekommen wäre.

Now he had heard that the Queen was so gracious, because
she had also come from poor peasants.

2.9 Da ging er zu ihr, und bat sie, ob sie ihm nicht helfen
könnte, daß er sein Füllchen wieder bekäme.

So he went to her and asked her if she could not help him to
get his cornucopia back.

2.10 Sagte sie:

She said,

2.11 »Ja, wenn Ihr mir versprecht, daß Ihr mich nicht
verraten wollt, so will ich's Euch sagen.

"Yes, if you will promise me that you will not betray me, I
will tell you.

Morgen früh, wenn der König auf der Wachtparade 2.12
ist, so stellt Euch hin, mitten in die Straße, wo er
vorbeikommen muß, nehmt ein großes Fischgarn
und thut, als fischtet Ihr, und fischt also fort und
schüttet das Garn aus, als wenn Ihr's voll hättet.«
Tomorrow morning, when the King is on the watch-parade,
stand in the middle of the road, where he must pass, take a
large fishing-net, and pretend to fish, and so fish away, and
pour out the net as if you had it full."

und sagte ihm auch was er antworten sollte, wenn er 2.13
vom König gefragt würde.
and told him what he should answer if he were asked by the
King.

Also stand der Bauer am anderen Tage da und fischte 2.14
auf einem trockenen Platze.
So the farmer stood there the next day and fished in a dry
place.

Wie der König vorbeikam und das sah, schickte 2.15
er seinen Läufer hin, der sollte fragen, was der
närrische Mann vor hätte.
When the king came by and saw this, he sent his bishop to
ask what the foolish man was up to.

Da gab er zur Antwort: »Ich fische.« 2.16
He replied: "I'm fishing."

Fragte der Läufer, wie er fischen könnte, es wäre ja 2.17
kein Wasser da.
The runner asked how he could fish, as there was no water.

Sagte der Bauer: 2.18
The farmer said:

»So gut als zwei Ochsen können ein Füllen kriegen, 2.19
"As well as two oxen can get a fill,

2.20 so gut kann ich auch auf dem trockenen Platze
fischen.«

I can also fish on the dry place."

2.21 Der Läufer ging hin und brachte dem König die
Antwort, da ließ er den Bauer vor sich kommen,
und sagte ihm, das hätte er nicht von sich, von wem
er das hätte, und sollt's gleich bekennen.

The runner went and brought the king the answer, and he
had the farmer come before him, and told him that he had
not got it from himself, from whom he had got it, and that
he should confess it at once.

2.22 Der Bauer aber wollt's nicht thun und sagte immer,
Gott bewahr!

But the peasant would not do it, and always said, God
forbid!

2.23 er hätt' es von sich!

he had it from himself!

2.24 Sie legten ihn aber auf ein Gebund Stroh und
schlugen und drangsalten ihn so lange, bis er's
bekannte, daß er's von der Frau Königin hätte.

But they laid him on a bundle of straw and beat and
tortured him until he confessed that he had it from the
Queen.

2.25 Als der König nach Haus kam, sagte er zu seiner Frau,

When the King came home, he said to his wife,

2.26 »Warum bist du so falsch mit mir,

"Why are you so false to me,

2.27 ich will dich nicht mehr zur Gemahlin;

I no longer want you as my wife;

121

deine Zeit ist um, geh' wieder hin, woher du   2.28
gekommen bist, in dein Bauernhäuschen.«
your time is up, go back to where you came from, to your
little farmhouse."

Doch erlaubte er ihr eins, sie sollte sich das Liebste   2.29
und Beste mitnehmen was sie wüßte, und das sollte
ihr Abschied sein.
But he allowed her one thing: she was to take with her the
dearest and best thing she knew, and that was to be her
farewell.

Sie sagte: 2.30
She said,

»Ja, lieber Mann, wenn du's so befiehlst, will ich es   2.31
auch thun.«
"Yes, dear husband, if you say so, I will do it too."

und fiel über ihn her und küßte ihn und sprach, sie   2.32
wollte Abschied von ihm nehmen.
and fell upon him and kissed him and said she wanted to
say good-bye to him.

Dann ließ sie einen starken Schlaftrunk kommen,   2.33
Abschied mit ihm zu trinken:
Then she sent for a strong nightcap to drink farewell with
him:

der König that einen großen Zug, sie aber trank nur   2.34
ein wenig.
the king took a large draught, but she drank only a little.

2.35 Da geriet er bald in einen tiefen Schlaf und als sie das sah, rief sie einen Bedienten und nahm ein schönes weißes Linnentuch und schlug ihn da hinein, und die Bedienten mußten ihn in einen Wagen vor die Thür tragen, und fuhr sie ihn heim in ihr Häuschen.

He soon fell into a deep sleep, and when she saw this, she called a servant and took a beautiful white linen cloth and wrapped him in it, and the servants had to carry him in a carriage to the door, and she drove him home to her little house.

2.36 Da legte sie ihn in ihr Bettchen, und er schlief Tag und Nacht in einem fort, und als er aufwachte, sah er sich um, und sagte,

Then she laid him down in her little bed, and he slept day and night in a row, and when he woke up he looked round, and said,

2.37 »Ach Gott, wo bin ich denn?« rief seinen Bedienten,

"Oh, God, where am I?" and called his servants,

2.38 aber es war keiner da.

but there was no one there.

2.39 Endlich kam seine Frau vor's Bett und sagte:

At last his wife came to his bedside and said,

2.40 »Lieber Herr König, Ihr habt mir befohlen, ich sollte das Liebste und Beste aus dem Schloß mitnehmen, nun hab ich nichts Besseres und Lieberes als dich, da hab ich dich mitgenommen!«

"Dear Sir King, you ordered me to take the best and dearest things from the castle, and now I have nothing better and dearer than you, so I have taken you with me!"

2.41 Dem König stiegen die Thränen in die Augen und er sagte,

The king's eyes filled with tears, and he said,

»Liebe Frau, du sollst mein sein und ich dein.« 2.42

"Dear wife, you shall be mine and I yours."

und nahm sie wieder mit ins königliche Schloß und 2.43
ließ sich aufs neue mit ihr vermählen;

and took her back to the royal palace and married her
anew;

und werden sie ja wohl noch auf den heutigen Tag 2.44
leben.

and they will probably live to this day.

Das Hausgesinde

The Household Servants

1.1 »Wo wust du henne?«
"Where do you want to go?"

1.2 »Nah Walpe.«
"Nah Walpe."

1.3 »Ick nah Walpe, du nah Walpe; sam, sam, goh wie dann.«
"Ick nah Walpe, du nah Walpe; sam, sam, goh wie dann."

2.1 »Häst du auck 'n Mann? Wie hedd din Mann?«
"Do you have a husband? What's your husband like?"

2.2 »Cham.«
"Cham."

2.3 »Min Mann Cham, din Mann Cham: ick nah Walpe,
"My husband Cham, your husband Cham: I'm close to Walpe,

2.4 du nah Walpe; sam, sam, goh wie dann.«
you're close to Walpe; sam, sam, go like then."

»Häst du auck 'n Kind? Wie hedd din Kind?« 3.1
"Do you have a child? How's your child?"

»Grind.« 3.2
"Grind."

»Min Kind Grind, din Kind Grind: min Mann Cham, 3.3
din Mann Cham:
"Min child Grind, din child Grind: min man Cham, din
man Cham:

ick nah Walpe, du nah Walpe: sam, sam, goh wie 3.4
dann.«
ick nah Walpe, du nah Walpe: sam, sam, goh wie dann."

»Häst du auck 'ne Weige? Wie hedd dine Weige?« 4.1
"Do you also have a weige? How do you have your weige?"

»Hippodeige.« Mine Weige Hippodeige, dine Weige 4.2
Hippodeige:
"Hippodeige." Mine Weige Hippodeige, dine Weige
Hippodeige:

min Kind Grind, din Kind Grind: min Mann Cham, 4.3
din Mann Cham:
min Kind Grind, din Kind Grind: min Mann Cham, din
Mann Cham:

ick nah Walpe, du nah Walpe: sam, sam, goh wie 4.4
dann.«
ick nah Walpe, du nah Walpe: sam, sam, goh wie dann."

»Häst du auck 'n Knecht? Wie hedd din Knecht?« 5.1
"Do you have a servant? How did your servant?"

»Machmirsrecht.« 5.2
"Machmirsrecht."

5.3 »Min Knecht Machmirsrecht, din Knecht Machmirsrecht:

"Min servant Machmirsrecht, din servant Machmirsrecht:

5.4 mine Weige Hippodeige, dine Weige Hippodeige: min Kind Grind,

mine Weige Hippodeige, dine Weige Hippodeige: min Kind Grind,

5.5 din Kind Grind: min Mann Cham, din Mann Cham; ick nah Walpe,

din Kind Grind: min Mann Cham, din Mann Cham; ick nah Walpe,

5.6 du nah Walpe; sam, sam, goh wie dann.«

du nah Walpe; sam, sam, goh wie dann."

Das Lämmchen und Fischchen

The Little Lamb and the Little Fish

1.1 **Es war ein Brüderchen und ein Schwesterchen, die hatten sich herzlich lieb.**

There was a little brother and a little sister who loved each other dearly.

1.2 **Ihre rechte Mutter war aber tot, und sie hatten eine Stiefmutter, die war ihnen nicht gut und that ihnen heimlich alles Leid an.**

But their real mother was dead, and they had a stepmother who was not good to them, and secretly did them all harm.

1.3 **Es trug sich zu, daß die zwei mit anderen Kindern auf einer Wiese vor dem Hause spielten, und an der Wiese war ein Teich, der ging bis an die eine Seite vom Hause.**

It happened that the two were playing with other children in a meadow in front of the house, and by the meadow was a pond which went up to one side of the house.

Die Kinder liefen da herum, kriegten sich und spielten Abzählens: 1.4
The children were running about there, getting into fights, and playing at counting:

»Eneke, Beneke, lat mi liewen,	"Eneke, Beneke, lat mi liewen,
will di ock min Vügelken giewen.	will also give you my wings.
Vügelken sall mi Strau söken,	Vügelken should give me strength,
Strau will ick den Köseken giewen,	Strau will ick den Köseken giewen,
Köseken sall mie Melk giewen,	Köseken should go to Melk,
Melk will ick den Bäcker giewen,	I want to go to the bakery,
Bäcker sall mie 'n Kocken backen,	Bakers should bake me a cake,
Kocken will ick den Kätken giewen,	I want to cook the cheese,
Kätken sall mie Müse fangen,	Kätken sall mie Müse fangen,
Müse will ick in 'n Rauck hangen	I want to hang in a smoke
un will se anschnien.«	un will se anschnien."

3.1 Dabei standen sie in einem Kreis, und auf welchen nun das Wort

They stood in a circle, and whoever was called

3.2 »anschnien«

"anschnien"

3.3 fiel, der mußte fortlaufen und die anderen liefen ihm nach und fingen ihn.

had to run away and the others ran after him and caught him.

3.4 Wie sie so fröhlich dahinsprangen,

As they leaped along so merrily,

3.5 sah's die Stiefmutter vom Fenster mit an und ärgerte sich.

the stepmother saw them from the window and was annoyed.

3.6 Weil sie aber Hexenkünste verstand, so verwünschte sie beide:

But because she knew witchcraft, she cursed them both:

3.7 das Brüderchen in einen Fisch und das Schwesterchen in ein Lamm.

the little brother into a fish and the little sister into a lamb.

3.8 Da schwamm das Fischchen im Teich hin und her, und war traurig, das Lämmchen ging auf der Wiese hin und her, und war traurig und fraß nicht und rührte kein Hälmchen an.

So the little fish swam to and fro in the pond and was sad, the little lamb walked to and fro in the meadow and was sad and did not eat or touch a stalk.

3.9 So ging eine lange Zeit hin,

So a long time passed,

da kamen fremde Gäste auf das Schloß.   3.10
and then strange guests came to the castle.

Die falsche Stiefmutter dachte,   3.11
The false stepmother thought,

»Jetzt ist die Gelegenheit gut.«   3.12
"Now is a good time."

rief den Koch und sprach zu ihm: 3.13
She called the cook and said to him,

»Geh und hol das Lamm von der Wiese und   3.14
schlacht's,
"Go and fetch the lamb from the meadow and slaughter it,

wir haben sonst nichts für die Gäste.«   3.15
we have nothing else for the guests."

Da ging der Koch hin und holte das Lämmchen und   3.16
führte es in die Küche und band ihm die Füßchen;
So the cook went and fetched the little lamb and led it into
the kitchen and tied its feet;

das litt es alles geduldig.   3.17
it suffered all this patiently.

Wie er nun sein Messer herausgezogen hatte und auf   3.18
der Schwelle wetzte, um es abzustechen, sah es, wie
ein Fischlein in dem Wasser vor dem Gossenstein hin
und her schwamm und zu ihm hinaufblickte.
When he had drawn out his knife, and was sharpening it
on the threshold to cut it off, he saw a little fish swimming
to and fro in the water in front of the watering-place, and
looking up at him.

132

3.19 **Das war aber das Brüderchen, denn als das Fischchen gesehen hatte wie der Koch das Lämmchen fortführte, war es Teich mitgeschwommen bis zum Haus.**

But it was the little brother, for when the little fish had seen the cook leading the lamb away, it had swum along in the pond as far as the house.

3.20 **Da rief das Lämmchen hinab:**

Then the little lamb called down:

»Ach Brüderchen im tiefen See,	"Oh little brother in the deep lake,
wie thut mir doch mein Herz so weh!	how my heart hurts so much!
der Koch der wetzt das Messer,	the cook sharpens the knife,
will mir mein Herz durchstechen.«	wants to pierce my heart."

5.1 **Das Fischchen antwortete:**

The little fish replied:

»Ach Schwesterchen in der Höh,	"Oh, sister on high,
wie thut mir doch mein Herz so weh!	how my heart hurts so much!
In dieser tiefen See!«	In this deep sea!"

Wie der Koch hörte, daß das Lämmchen sprechen   7.1
konnte und so traurige Worte zum Fischchen
hinabrief, erschrak er und dachte, es müßte kein
natürliches Lämmchen sein, sondern wäre von der
bösen Frau im Hause verwünscht.

When the cook heard that the little lamb could speak
and called down such sad words to the little fish, he was
frightened and thought that it must not be a natural lamb,
but was cursed by the wicked woman in the house.

Da sprach er: »Sei ruhig, ich will dich nicht   7.2
schlachten.«

Then he said, "Be quiet, I will not slaughter you."

nahm ein anderes Tier und bereitete das für die   7.3
Gäste, und brachte das Lämmchen zu einer guten
Bäuerin, der erzählte er alles, was er gesehen und
gehört hatte.

He took another animal and prepared it for the guests, and
took the lamb to a good farmer's wife, to whom he told
everything he had seen and heard.

Die Bäuerin war aber gerade die Amme von dem   7.4
Schwesterchen gewesen, vermutete gleich, wer's sein
würde und ging mit ihm zu einer weisen Frau.

But the farmer's wife had just been the nurse of the little
sister, and immediately guessed who it was, and went with
him to a wise woman.

7.5 Da sprach die Frau einen Segen über das Lämmchen und Fischchen, wovon sie ihre menschliche Gestalt wieder bekamen, und danach führte sie beide in einen großen Wald in ein kleines Häuschen, wo sie einsam, aber zufrieden und glücklich lebten.

The woman said a blessing over the little lamb and the little fish, which gave them back their human form, and then she took them both into a large forest to a little house, where they lived alone, but contented and happy.

Simeliberg

1.1 **Es waren zwei Brüder, einer war reich, der andere arm.**
There were two brothers, one rich, the other poor.

1.2 **Der Reiche aber gab dem Armen nichts,**
But the rich one gave nothing to the poor one,

1.3 **und er mußte sich vom Kornhandel kümmerlich ernähren;**
and he had to feed himself miserably from the corn trade;

1.4 **da ging es ihm oft so schlecht, daß er für seine Frau und Kinder kein Brot hatte.**
and he was often so badly off that he had no bread for his wife and children.

1.5 **Einmal fuhr er mit seinem Karren durch den Wald, da erblickte er zur Seite einen großen kahlen Berg, und weil er den noch nie gesehen hatte, hielt er still und betrachtete ihn mit Verwunderung.**
Once he was driving his cart through the forest, when he saw a great bare mountain to one side, and as he had never seen it before, he stood still and looked at it in amazement.

Wie er so stand, sah er zwölf wilde große Männner daher kommen; weil er nun glaubte, das wären Räuber, schob er seinen Karren ins Gebüsch und stieg auf einen Baum und wartete, was da geschehen würde.

1.6

As he stood there, he saw twelve tall wild men coming towards him, and thinking they were robbers, he pushed his cart into the bushes and climbed a tree and waited to see what would happen.

Die zwölf Männer gingen aber vor den Berg und riefen:

1.7

The twelve men went to the mountain and shouted:

»Berg Semsi, Berg Semsi, thu dich auf.«

1.8

"Mount Semsi, Mount Semsi, open up."

Alsbald that sich der kahle Berg in der Mitte voneinander, und die zwölfe gingen hinein, und wie sie drin waren, schloß er sich zu.

1.9

Immediately the bare mountain parted in the middle, and the twelve men went in, and as soon as they were inside, it closed.

Über eine kleine Weile that er sich wieder auf und die Männer kamen heraus und trugen schwere Säcke auf den Rücken, und wie sie alle wieder am Tageslicht waren, sprachen sie,

1.10

After a little while it opened again, and the men came out carrying heavy sacks on their backs, and when they were all in the daylight again, they said,

»Berg Semsi, Berg Semsi, thu dich zu.«

1.11

"Mount Semsi, Mount Semsi, close up."

1.12 Da fuhr der Berg zusammen und war kein Eingang
mehr an ihm zu sehen,
Then the mountain collapsed and there was no longer any
entrance to it,

1.13 und die zwölfe gingen fort.
and the twelve went away.

1.14 Als sie ihm nun ganz aus den Augen waren, stieg der
Arme vom Baum herunter, und war neugierig, was
wohl im Berge Heimliches verborgen wäre.
When they were quite out of sight of it, the poor man came
down from the tree, and was curious to know what secret
things were hidden in the mountain.

1.15 Also ging er davor und sprach,
So he went before it and said,

1.16 »Berg Semsi, Berg Semsi, thu dich auf.«
"Mount Semsi, Mount Semsi, open up."

1.17 und der Berg that sich auch vor ihm auf.
and the mountain opened up before him.

1.18 Da trat er hinein, und der ganze Berg war eine
Höhle voll Silber und Gold, und hinten lagen große
Haufen Perlen und blitzende Edelsteine wie Korn
aufgeschüttet.
Then he went in, and the whole mountain was a cave full of
silver and gold, and at the back were great heaps of pearls
and glittering precious stones heaped up like grain.

1.19 Der Arme wußte gar nicht was er anfangen sollte und
ob er sich etwas von den Schätzen nehmen dürfte;
The poor man did not know what to do or whether he
should take any of the treasures;

endlich füllte er sich die Taschen mit Gold, 1.20
at last he filled his pockets with gold,

die Perlen und Edelsteine aber ließ er liegen. 1.21
but left the pearls and precious stones behind.

Als er wieder herauskam, sprach er gleichfalls: 1.22
When he came out again, he also said:

»Berg Semsi, Berg Semsi, thu dich zu.« 1.23
"Mount Semsi, Mount Semsi, close up."

da schloß sich der Berg und er fuhr mit seinem 1.24
Karren nach Hause.
Then the mountain closed and he drove home in his cart.

Nun brauchte er nicht mehr zu sorgen und konnte 1.25
mit seinem Golde für Frau und Kind Brot und auch
Wein dazu kaufen, lebte fröhlich und redlich, gab den
Armen und that jedermann Gutes.
Now he no longer needed to worry and was able to buy
bread and wine for his wife and child with his gold, lived
happily and honestly, gave to the poor and did good to
everyone.

Als aber das Geld zu Ende war, ging er zu seinem 1.26
Bruder, lieh einen Scheffel und holte sich von neuem;
doch rührte er von den großen Schätzen nichts an.
But when the money ran out, he went to his brother,
borrowed a bushel and got some more, but he did not
touch any of the great treasures.

Wie er sich zum drittenmal etwas holen wollte, 1.27
When he wanted to get something for the third time,

borgte er bei seinem Bruder abermals den Scheffel. 1.28
he borrowed the bushel from his brother again.

140

1.29 **Der Reiche aber war schon lange neidisch über sein Vermögen und den schönen Haushalt, den er sich eingerichtet hatte, und konnte nicht begreifen woher der Reichtum käme und was sein Bruder mit dem Scheffel anfinge.**

The rich man, however, had long been envious of his wealth and the beautiful household he had set up for himself, and could not understand where the wealth came from and what his brother was doing with the bushel.

1.30 **Da dachte er eine List aus und bestrich den Boden mit Pech, und wie er das Maß zurückbekam, so war ein Goldstück darin hängen geblieben.**

So he thought up a trick and coated the ground with pitch, and when he got the measure back, a piece of gold had got stuck in it.

1.31 **Alsbald ging er zu seinem Bruder und fragte ihn:**

He immediately went to his brother and asked him:

1.32 **»Was hast du mit dem Scheffel gemessen?«**

"What did you measure with the bushel?"

1.33 **»Korn und Gerste.« sagte der andere.**

"Corn and barley." said the other.

1.34 **Da zeigte er ihm das Goldstück und drohte ihm, wenn er, nicht die Wahrheit sagte, so wollte er ihn beim Gericht verklagen.**

Then he showed him the piece of gold and threatened him that if he did not tell the truth, he would sue him in court.

1.35 **Er erzählte, ihm nun alles, wie es zugegangen war.**

So he told him everything that had happened.

Der Reiche aber ließ gleich einen Wagen anspannen, 1.36
fuhr hinaus, wollte die Gelegenheit besser benutzen
und ganz andere Schätze mitbringen.
But the rich man immediately had a wagon hitched up and
drove out, wanting to make better use of the opportunity
and bring back completely different treasures.

Wie er vor den Berg kam, rief er: 1.37
When he came to the mountain, he called out:

»Berg Semsi, Berg Semsi, thu dich auf.« 1.38
"Mount Semsi, Mount Semsi, open up."

Der Berg that sich auf, und er ging hinein. 1.39
The mountain opened up and he went inside.

Da lagen die Reichtümer alle vor ihm, und er wußte 1.40
lange nicht, wozu er am ersten greifen sollte, endlich
lud er Edelsteine auf, so viel er tragen konnte.
All the riches lay before him, and for a long time he did
not know what to reach for first, but at last he loaded up as
many precious stones as he could carry.

Er wollte seine Last hinausbringen, weil aber Herz 1.41
und Sinn ganz voll von den Schätzen waren, hatte er
darüber den Namen des Berges vergessen, und rief:
He wanted to take his load out, but because his heart and
mind were full of the treasures, he had forgotten the name
of the mountain and called out:

»Berg Simeli, Berg Simeli, thu dich auf.« 1.42
"Mount Simeli, Mount Simeli, open up."

Aber das war der rechte Name nicht, 1.43
But that was not the right name,

und der Berg regte sich nicht und blieb verschlossen. 1.44
and the mountain did not move and remained closed.

1.45 Da ward ihm angst, aber je länger er nachsann, desto mehr verwirrten sich seine Gedanken, und halfen ihm alle Schätze nichts mehr.

He was frightened, but the longer he pondered, the more confused his thoughts became, and all his treasures were of no use to him.

1.46 Am Abend that sich der Berg auf und die zwölf Räuber kamen herein, und als sie ihn sahen, lachten sie und riefen:

In the evening the mountain opened, and the twelve robbers came in, and when they saw him they laughed and cried,

1.47 »Vogel, haben wir dich endlich, meinst du, wir hätten's nicht gemerkt, daß du zweimal hereingekommen bist, aber wir konnten dich nicht fangen, zum drittenmal sollst du nicht wieder heraus.«

"Bird, we have got you at last, do you think we did not realize that you came in twice, but we could not catch you, and you shall not come out the third time."

1.48 Da rief er: »Ich war's nicht, mein Bruder war's.«

Then he cried, "It was not I, it was my brother."

1.49 aber er mochte bitten um sein Leben und sagen was er wollte,

but he might plead for his life and say what he liked,

1.50 sie schlugen ihm das Haupt ab.

but they cut off his head.

Up Reisen gohn

Up Traveling Gohn

1.1 **Et was emol 'ne arme Frau, de hadde enen Suhn, de wull so gerne reisen, do seg de Mohr:**
There was once a poor woman who had a son who wanted to travel so much that the mother said:

1.2 **»Wu kannst du reisen?**
"How can you travel?

1.3 **wi hebt je gar kien Geld, dat du mitniemen kannst.«**
We don't have any money that you can take with you."

1.4 **Do seg de Suhn: »Ick will mi gut behelpen,**
Then the son said: "I want to help myself well,

1.5 **ick will alltied seggen: Nig viel, nig viel, nig viel.«**
I want to say everything: Not much, not much, not much."

2.1 **Do genk he ene gude Tied un sede alltied:**
Then he had a good time and sang all the time:

2.2 **»Nig viel, nig viel, nig viel.«**
"Not much, not much, not much."

Kam do bi en Trop Fisker un seg: »Gott helpe ju!   2.3
He came across a drop of fish and said: "God help me!

nig viel, nig viel, nig viel.«   2.4
not much, not much, not much."

»Wat segst du, Kerl, nig viel?«   2.5
"What are you saying, guy, not much?"

Un asse dat Gören (Garn) uttrocken,   2.6
And when they dried out the yarn,

kregen se auck nig viel Fiske. So met enen Stock up de   2.7
Jungen,
they also got a few fish. So with a stick on the boy,

un: »Hest du mig nig dresken (dreschen) seihn?«   2.8
and: "Have you seen a little bit of threshing?"

»Wat sall ick denn seggen?« seg de Junge.   2.9
"What should I say?" said the boy.

»Du sallst seggen: Fank vull, fank vull.«   2.10
"You should say: Fank vull, fank vull."

Do geit he wier ene ganze Tied un seg: »Fank vull,   3.1
Then he goes on for a whole day and says: "Fank vull,

fank vull.«   3.2
fank vull."

bis he kümmt an enen Galgen, do hebt se en armen   3.3
Sünder, den willt se richten.
Until he comes to a gallows, where she picks up a poor
sinner, whom she wants to judge.

3.4 Do seg he: »Guden Morgen, fank vull, fank vull.«
Then he sings: "Good morning, full, full, full."

3.5 »Wat segst du, Kerl, fank vull?
"What do you say, guy, full?

3.6 Söllt der noch mehr leige (leidige, böse) Lüde in de Welt sien?
Should there be any more leige (sorry, evil) Lüde in the world?

3.7 Is düt noch nig genog?« He krig wier wat up den Puckel.
Is that still not enough?" He got something on his puck.

3.8 »Wat sall ick denn seggen?« Du sallst seggen:
"What should I say then?" You have to say:

3.9 Gott tröst de arme Seele.«
God comforts the poor soul."

4.1 De Junge geit wier ene ganze Tied un seg:
The boy goes on for a whole day and says:

4.2 »Gott tröst de arme Seele!«
"God comfort the poor soul!"

4.3 Da kümmet he an en Grawen, do steit en Filler (Schinder), de tüt en Perd af.
Then he comes to a grave, where a filler is standing, who is carrying a pearl.

4.4 De Junge seg: »Guden Morgen, Gott tröst de arme Seele!«
The boy says: "Good morning, God comfort the poor soul!"

»Wat segst du, leige Kerl?«   4.5
"What are you saying, little fellow?"

un schleit en met sinen Filhacken üm de Ohren,   4.6
and he slides his felt hooks around his ears,

da he ut den Augen nig seihen kann.   4.7
as he can't see out of his eyes.

»Wu sall ick denn seggen?«   4.8
"What should I say then?"

»Du sallst seggen: Do ligge du Aas in en Grawen.«   4.9
"You have to say it: You're lying in a grave."

Do geit he und seg alltied: 5.1
Then he goes and says to everyone:

»Do ligge du Aas in en Grawen! Do ligge du Aas in en   5.2
Grawen!«
"You're lying in a grave! You're lying in a grave!"

Nu kümmt he bi enen Wagen vull Lüde, do seg he: 5.3
Now he comes to a wagon full of people, then he says:

»Guden Morgen, do ligge du Aas in en Grawen!«   5.4
"Good morning, you're lying in a grave!"

Do föllt de Wagen üm in en Grawen, de Knecht kreg   5.5
de Pietske un knapt den Jungen, dat he wier to sine
Mohr krupen moste.
Then the wagon falls over into a ditch, the servant grabs the
pie mask and bends the boy over so that he has to go back to
his mother.

5.6 **Un he is sien Lewen nig wier up Reisen gohn.**
And he went on his travels again.

Das Eselein
The Little Donkey

1.1 Es lebte einmal ein König und eine Königin, die waren reich und hatten alles, was sie sich wünschten, nur keine Kinder.

Once upon a time there lived a king and queen who were rich and had everything they could wish for, but no children.

1.2 Darüber klagte sie Tag und Nacht und sprach:

She complained about this day and night, saying:

1.3 »Ich bin wie ein Acker, auf dem nichts wächst.«

"I am like a field where nothing grows."

1.4 Endlich erfüllte Gott ihre Wünsche:

At last God fulfilled her wishes:

1.5 als das Kind aber zur Welt kam, sah's nicht aus wie ein Menschenkind, sondern war ein junges Eselein.

but when the child was born, it did not look like a human child, but was a young donkey.

Wie die Mutter das erblickte, fing ihr Jammer und
Geschrei erst recht an, sie hätte lieber gar kein Kind
gehabt als einen Esel, und sagte, man sollte ihn ins
Wasser werfen, damit ihn die Fische fräßen.

1.6

When the mother saw this, her wailing and crying began
all the more; she would rather have had no child at all than
a donkey, and said that it should be thrown into the water
for the fish to eat.

Der König aber sprach:

1.7

But the king said,

»Nein, hat Gott ihn gegeben, soll er auch mein
Sohn und Erbe sein, nach meinem Tode auf dem
königlichen Thron sitzen und die königliche Krone
tragen.«

1.8

"No, if God has given him, he shall be my son and heir, and
after my death he shall sit on the royal throne and wear the
royal crown."

Also ward das Eselein aufgezogen, nahm zu, und
die Ohren wuchsen ihm auch fein hoch und gerad
hinauf.

1.9

So the little donkey was reared, grew up, and his ears grew
high and straight.

Es war aber sonst fröhlicher Art, sprang herum,
spielte und hatte besonders seine Lust an der Musik,
sodaß es zu einem berühmten Spielmann ging und
sprach,

1.10

But he was otherwise cheerful, jumped about, played, and
was particularly fond of music, so that he went to a famous
minstrel, and said,

»Lehre mich deine Kunst,

1.11

"Teach me your art,

152

1.12 daß ich so gut die Laute schlagen kann als du.«
that I may play the lute as well as you."

1.13 »Ach, liebes Herrlein.« antwortete der Spielmann,
"Oh, dear sir." replied the minstrel,

1.14 »das sollt Euch schwer fallen,
"that should be difficult for you,

1.15 Eure Finger sind allerdings nicht dazu gemacht und gar zu groß;
but your fingers are not made for it and are too big;

1.16 ich sorge, die Saiten halten's nicht aus.«
I'm afraid the strings won't hold out."

1.17 Es half keine Ausrede, das Eselein wollte und mußte die Laute schlagen, war beharrlich und fleißig und lernte es am Ende so gut als sein Meister selber.
No excuses helped, the little donkey wanted and had to play the lute, was persistent and diligent and in the end learned it as well as his master himself.

1.18 Einmal ging das junge Herrlein nachdenksam spazieren und kam an einen Brunnen,
Once the young master went for a thoughtful walk and came to a fountain,

1.19 da schaute es hinein und sah im spiegelhellen Wasser seine Eseleinsgestalt.
where he looked in and saw the figure of his little donkey in the mirror-bright water.

1.20 Darüber war es so betrübt,
He was so saddened by this that he went out into the wide world,

daß es in die weite Welt ging und nur einen treuen   1.21
Gesellen mitnahm.
taking only one faithful companion with him.

Sie zogen auf und ab, zuletzt kamen sie in ein Reich,   1.22
wo ein alter König herrschte, der nur eine einzige
aber wunderschöne Tochter hatte.
They traveled up and down and finally came to a kingdom
where an old king ruled who had only one beautiful
daughter.

Das Eselein sagte: »Hier wollen wir weilen.«   1.23
The little donkey said, "Here we will dwell."

klopfte ans Thor und rief: 1.24
knocked at the gate, and cried,

»Es ist ein Gast haußen, macht auf, damit er eingehen   1.25
kann.«
"There is a guest outside, open the door that he may enter."

Als aber nicht aufgethan ward, setzte er sich hin,   1.26
nahm seine Laute und schlug sie mit seinen zwei
Vorderfüßen aufs lieblichste.
But when the door was not opened, he sat down, took his
lute, and beat it most sweetly with his two forefeet.

Da sperrte der Thürhüter gewaltig die Augen auf, lief   1.27
zum König und sprach,
Then the doorkeeper opened his eyes wide, ran to the king,
and said,

»Da draußen sitzt ein junges Eselein vor dem Thor,   1.28
"There is a young donkey sitting outside the gate,

das schlägt die Laute so gut als ein gelernter Meister.«   1.29
who plays the lute as well as a skilled master."

1.30 »So laß mir den Musikanten hereinkommen.« sprach der König.
"Let the musician come in." said the king.

1.31 Wie aber ein Eselein hereintrat,
But when the little donkey came in,

1.32 fing alles an über den Lautenschläger zu lachen.
everyone began to laugh at the lute-player.

1.33 Nun sollte das Eselein, unten zu den Knechten gesetzt und gespeist werden, es ward aber unwillig und sprach,
Now the little donkey was to be seated downstairs with the servants and fed, but it became indignant and said,

1.34 »Ich bin kein gemeines Stalleselein, ich bin ein vornehmes.«
"I am not a common stable boy, I am a noble one."

1.35 Da sagten sie: »Wenn du das bist,
Then they said, "If that is what you are,

1.36 so setze dich zu dem Kriegsvolk.«
sit down with the soldiers."

1.37 »Nein.« sprach es, »ich will beim König sitzen.«
"No." said he, "I will sit with the king."

1.38 Der König lachte und sprach in gutem Mut:
The king laughed and said in good courage,

1.39 »Ja, es soll so sein, wie du verlangst, Eselein, komm her zu mir.«
"Yes, it shall be as you ask, little donkey, come here to me."

Danach fragte er: »Eselein, 1.40
Then he asked: "Little donkey,

wie gefällt dir meine Tochter?« 1.41
how do you like my daughter?"

Das Eselein drehte den Kopf nach ihr, schaute sie an, 1.42
nickte und sprach:
The little donkey turned his head towards her, looked at
her, nodded and said:

»Über die Maßen wohl, sie ist so schön wie ich noch 1.43
keine gesehen habe.«
"She is more beautiful than I have ever seen."

»Nun, so sollst du auch neben ihr sitzen.« sagte der 1.44
König.
"Well, you shall sit next to her." said the king.

»Das ist mir eben recht.« 1.45
"That is just as well for me."

sprach das Eselein und setzte sich an ihre Seite, aß 1.46
und trank und wußte sich fein und säuberlich zu
betragen.
said the little donkey, and sat down by her side, ate and
drank, and knew how to behave in a fine and neat manner.

Als das edle Tierlein eine gute Zeit an des Königs Hof 1.47
geblieben war, dachte es,
When the noble little animal had stayed a good while at the
King's court, he thought,

»Was hilft das alles, du mußt wieder heim.« 1.48
"What good is all this, you must go home again."

1.49 ließ den Kopf traurig hängen,

He hung his head sadly,

1.50 trat vor den König und verlangte seinen Abschied.

stood before the king and demanded his departure.

1.51 Der König hatte es aber lieb gewonnen und sprach: »Eselein,

But the king had grown fond of him and said, "Little donkey,

1.52 was ist dir?

what is the matter with you?

1.53 Du schaust ja sauer wie ein Essigkrug, bleib bei mir, ich will dir geben, was du verlangst.

You look as sour as a jug of vinegar, stay with me, I will give you what you ask for.

1.54 Willst du Gold?«

Do you want gold?"

1.55 »Nein.« sagte das Eselein und schüttelte mit dem Kopf.

"No." said the little donkey, shaking his head.

1.56 »Willst du Kostbarkeiten und Schmuck?«

"Do you want valuables and jewelry?"

1.57 »Nein.«

"No."

1.58 »Willst du mein halbes Reich?«

"Do you want half my kingdom?"

1.59 »Ach nein.« Da sprach der König,

"Oh no." Then the king said,

»Wenn ich nur wüßte, was dich vergnügt machen könnte: 1.60
"If only I knew what would make you happy:

willst du meine schöne Tochter zur Frau?« 1.61
do you want my beautiful daughter as your wife?"

»Ach ja.« sagte das Eselein, 1.62
"Oh yes." said the little donkey,

»die möchte ich wohl haben.« 1.63
"I should like to have her."

war auf einmal ganz lustig und guter Dinge, denn das war's gerade, was es sich gewünscht hatte. 1.64
All at once he was quite merry and in good spirits, for that was just what he had wished for.

Also ward eine große und prächtige Hochzeit gehalten. 1.65
So a great and splendid wedding was held.

Abends, wie Braut und Bräutigam in ihr Schlafkämmerlein geführt wurden, wollte der König wissen ob sich das Eselein auch sein artig und manierlich betrüge, und hieß einem Diener sich dort Verstecken. 1.66
In the evening, when the bride and bridegroom were led to their bedchamber, the king wanted to know whether the little donkey was also behaving well and in good manners, and ordered a servant to hide there.

1.67 Wie sie nun beide drinnen waren, schob der Bräutigam den Riegel vor die Thür, blickte sich um, und wie er glaubte, daß sie ganz allein wären, da warf er auf einmal seine Eselshaut ab und stand da als ein schöner königlicher Jüngling.

When they were both inside, the bridegroom pushed the bolt in front of the door, looked around, and as he thought they were quite alone, he suddenly threw off his donkey skin and stood there as a handsome royal youth.

1.68 »Nun siehst du.« sprach er,

"Now you see." said he,

1.69 »wer ich bin, und siehst auch, daß ich deiner nicht unwert war.«

"who I am, and see also that I was not unworthy of you."

1.70 Da ward die Braut froh, küßte ihn und hatte ihn von Herzen lieb.

Then the bride was glad, kissed him, and loved him dearly.

1.71 Als aber der Morgen herankam, sprang er auf, zog seine Tierhaut wieder über, und hätte kein Mensch gedacht, was für einer dahintersteckte.

But when morning came, he jumped up, put on his animal skin again, and no one would have guessed what sort of man was behind it.

1.72 Bald kam auch der alte König gegangen. »Ei.« rief er,

Soon the old king came out too. "Egg." he cried,

1.73 »ist das Eselein schon munter! Du bist wohl recht traurig.«

"the little donkey is already awake! You must be very sad."

1.74 sagte er zu seiner Tochter,

he said to his daughter,

»daß du keinen ordentlichen Menschen zum Mann bekommen hast?«   1.75

"that you have not got a proper man for a husband?"

»Ach nein, lieber Vater, ich habe ihn so lieb, als wenn er der allerschönste wäre, und will ihn mein Lebtag behalten.«   1.76

"Oh no, dear father, I love him as much as if he were the most beautiful, and I want to keep him all my life."

Der König wunderte sich, aber der Diener, der sich versteckt hatte, kam und offenbarte ihm alles.   1.77

The king was astonished, but the servant who had hidden himself came and revealed everything to him.

Der König sprach: »Das ist nimmermehr wahr.«   1.78

The king said, "That is never true."

»So wacht selber die folgende Nacht, ihr werdet's mit eigenen Augen sehen, und wißt ihr was, Herr König, nehmt ihm die Haut weg und werft sie ins Feuer, so muß er sich wohl in seiner rechten Gestalt zeigen.«   1.79

"So watch for yourselves the next night, you will see it with your own eyes, and you know what, Sir King, take away his skin and throw it into the fire, and he must show himself in his true form."

»Dein Rat ist gut.«   1.80

"Your advice is good."

sprach der König, und abends, als sie schliefen, schlich er sich hinein, und wie er zum Bett kam, sah er im Mondschein einen stolzen Jüngling da ruhen und die Haut lag abgestreift auf der Erde.   1.81

said the king, and in the evening, when they were asleep, he crept in, and when he came to the bed, he saw a proud youth resting there in the moonlight, and the skin lay stripped off on the ground.

1.82 **Da nahm er sie weg und ließ draußen ein gewaltiges Feuer anmachen und die Haut hineinwerfen, und blieb selber dabei, bis sie ganz zu Asche verbrannt war.**

So he took it away and had a huge fire lit outside and threw the skin into it, and stayed there himself until it was burnt to ashes.

1.83 **Weil er aber sehen wollte, wie sich der Beraubte anstellen würde, blieb er die Nacht über wach und lauschte.**

But because he wanted to see what the robbed man would do, he stayed awake all night and listened.

1.84 **Als der Jüngling ausgeschlafen hatte, beim ersten Morgenschein, stand er auf und wollte die Eselshaut anziehen, aber sie war nicht zu finden.**

When the young man had slept well, at the first light of dawn, he got up and wanted to put on the donkey skin, but it was not to be found.

1.85 **Da erschrak er und sprach voll Trauer und Angst,**

Then he was frightened, and said, full of grief and fear,

1.86 **»Nun muß ich sehen, daß ich entfliehe.«**

"Now I must see that I escape."

1.87 **Wie er hinaustrat, stand aber der König da und sprach,**

As he went out, the king stood there and said,

1.88 **»Mein Sohn, wohin so eilig, was hast du im Sinn?**

"My son, where are you going in such a hurry, what are you thinking of?

Bleib hier, du bist ein so schöner Mann, du sollst   1.89
nicht wieder von mir.
Stay here, you are such a handsome man, you shall not
leave me again.

Ich gebe dir jetzt mein Reich halb,   1.90
I give you half my kingdom now,

und nach meinem Tode bekommst du es ganz.«   1.91
and after my death you shall have it in full."

»So wünsch ich, daß der gute Anfang auch ein gutes   1.92
Ende nehme.«
"I wish that the good beginning may have a good end."

sprach der Jüngling, »ich bleibe bei Euch.«   1.93
said the youth, "I will stay with you."

Da gab ihm der Alte das halbe Reich, und als er nach   1.94
einem Jahr starb, hatte er das ganze, und nach dem
Tode seines Vaters noch eins dazu, und lebte in aller
Herrlichkeit.
So the old man gave him half the kingdom, and when he
died a year later he had the whole, and after his father's
death he had one more, and lived in all glory.

Der undankbare Sohn

The Ungrateful Son

1.1 Es saß einmal ein Mann mit seiner Frau vor der Hausthür,

Once a man and his wife were sitting at the door of their house,

1.2 und sie hatten ein gebraten Huhn vor sich stehen und wollten das zusammen verzehren.

and they had a roast chicken in front of them and wanted to eat it together.

1.3 Da sah der Mann, wie sein alter Vater daher kam, geschwind nahm er das Huhn und versteckte es, weil er ihm nichts davon gönnte.

Then the man saw his old father coming along, and he quickly took the chicken and hid it because he didn't want any of it.

1.4 Der Alte kam, that einen Trunk und ging fort.

The old man came, had a drink and went away.

Nun wollte der Sohn das gebratene Huhn wieder aus   1.5
den Tisch tragen, aber als er danach griff, war es eine
große Kröte geworden, die sprang ihm ins Angesicht
und saß da, und ging nicht wieder weg;

Now the son wanted to carry the roast chicken out of the
table again, but when he reached for it, it had become a
large toad, which jumped into his face and sat there, and
did not go away again;

und wenn sie jemand wegthun wollte, sah sie ihn   1.6
giftig an, als wollte sie ihm ins Gesicht springen,
sodaß keiner sie anzurühren getraute.

and when anyone wanted to take it away, it looked at him
venomously, as if it wanted to jump into his face, so that no
one dared to touch it.

Und die Kröte mußte der undankbare Sohn alle Tage   1.7
füttern,

And the ungrateful son had to feed the toad every day,

sonst fraß sie ihm aus seinem Angesicht;   1.8

otherwise it would eat out of his face;

und also ging er ohne Ruhe in der Welt hin und her.   1.9

and so he went to and fro in the world without rest.

Hänsel und Gretel

Hansel and Gretel

1.1 **Vor einem großen Walde wohnte ein armer Holzhacker mit seiner Frau und seinen zwei Kindern;**
Outside a large forest lived a poor woodcutter with his wife and two children;

1.2 **das Bübchen hieß Hänsel und das Mädchen Gretel.**
the boy was called Hansel and the girl Gretel.

1.3 **Er hatte wenig zu beißen und zu brechen, und einmal, als große Teuerung ins Land kam, konnte er auch das tägliche Brot nicht mehr schaffen.**
He had little to eat and little to break, and once, when great famine came to the land, he could no longer make his daily bread.

1.4 **Wie er sich nun abends im Bette Gedanken machte und sich vor Sorgen herumwälzte, seufzte er und sprach zu seiner Frau:**
As he lay in bed at night, tossing and turning with worry, he sighed and said to his wife:

1.5 **»Was soll aus uns werden?**
"What is to become of us?

Wie können wir unsere armen Kinder ernähren, da wir für uns selbst nichts mehr haben?«

How can we feed our poor children now that we have nothing left for ourselves?"

»Weißt du was, Mann.« antwortete die Frau,

"You know what, man." the wife replied,

»wir wollen morgen in aller Frühe die Kinder hinaus in den Wald führen, wo er am dicksten ist:

"tomorrow morning we'll take the children out into the forest where it's thickest:

da machen wir ihnen ein Feuer an und geben jedem noch ein Stückchen Brot,

we'll light a fire and give them each a piece of bread,

dann gehen wir an unsere Arbeit und lassen sie allein.

then we'll go to our work and leave them alone.

Sie finden den Weg nicht wieder nach Hause und wir sind sie los.«

They won't find their way home again and we'll be rid of them."

»Nein, Frau.« sagte der Mann, »das thue ich nicht;

"No, woman." said the man, "I won't do that;

wie sollte ich's übers Herz bringen, meine Kinder im Walde allein zu lassen, die wilden Tiere würden bald kommen und sie zerreißen.«

how could I have the heart to leave my children alone in the forest, the wild animals would soon come and tear them apart."

»O du Narr.« sagte sie,

"Oh, you fool." said she,

1.15 »dann müssen wir alle vier Hungers sterben, du kannst nur die Bretter für die Särge hobeln.«

"then we must all four die of hunger; you can only hew the boards for the coffins."

1.16 und ließ ihm keine Ruhe, bis er einwilligte.

and gave him no peace until he consented.

1.17 »Aber die armen Kinder dauern mich doch.« sagte der Mann.

"But the poor children will take me." said the man.

2.1 Die zwei Kinder hatten vor Hunger auch nicht einschlafen können und hatten gehört, was die Stiefmutter zum Vater gesagt hatte.

The two children had been so hungry that they could not sleep and had heard what the stepmother had said to their father.

2.2 Gretel weinte bittere Thränen und sprach zu Hänsel,

Gretel wept bitter tears and said to Hansel,

2.3 »Nun ist's um uns geschehen.«

"Now it's all over for us."

2.4 »Still, Gretel.« sprach Hänsel, »gräme dich nicht,

"Hush, Gretel." said Hansel, "do not grieve,

2.5 ich will uns schon helfen.«

I will help us."

2.6 Und als die Alten eingeschlafen waren, stand er auf, zog sein Röcklein an, machte die Unterthür auf und schlich sich hinaus.

And when the old people had fallen asleep, he got up, put on his little skirt, opened the under-door and crept out.

Da schien der Mond ganz hell, und die weißen 2.7
Kieselsteine, die vor dem Hause lagen, glänzten wie
lauter Batzen.
Then the moon was shining brightly, and the white pebbles
lying in front of the house were shining like a lot of lumps.

Hänsel bückte sich und steckte soviel in sein 2.8
Rocktäschlein, als nur hinein wollten.
Hansel stooped down and put as many as he wanted into his
little coat pocket.

Dann ging er wieder zurück, sprach zu Gretel: 2.9
Then he went back again, said to Gretel,

»Sei getrost, liebes Schwesterchen, und schlaf nur 2.10
ruhig ein, Gott wird uns nicht verlassen.«
"Take heart, dear little sister, and go to sleep quietly, God
will not forsake us."

und legte sich wieder in sein Bett. 2.11
and lay down again in his bed.

Als der Tag anbrach, noch ehe die Sonne aufgegangen 3.1
war, kam schon die Frau und weckte die beiden
Kinder:
When the day dawned, before the sun had even risen, the
woman came and woke the two children:

»Steht auf, ihr Faulenzer, wir wollen in den Wald 3.2
gehen und Holz holen.«
"Get up, you lazybones, we want to go into the forest and
fetch some wood."

Dann gab sie jedem ein Stückchen Brot und sprach: 3.3
Then she gave them each a piece of bread and said:

3.4 »Da habt ihr etwas für den Mittag, aber eßt nichts vorher auf, weiter kriegt ihr nichts.«

"Here's something for lunch, but don't eat anything first, you won't get anything else."

3.5 Gretel nahm das Brot unter die Schürze, weil Hänsel die Steine in der Tasche hatte.

Gretel took the bread under her apron because Hansel had the stones in his pocket.

3.6 Danach machten sie sich alle zusammen auf den Weg nach dem Walde.

Then they all set off together towards the forest.

3.7 Als sie ein Weilchen gegangen waren, stand Hänsel still, und guckte nach dem Hause zurück und that das wieder und immer wieder.

When they had walked for a while, Hansel stood still and looked back to the house and did this again and again.

3.8 Der Vater sprach:

His father said,

3.9 »Hänsel, was guckst du da und bleibst zurück, hab acht und vergiß deine Beine nicht.«

"Hansel, what are you looking at and staying behind, be careful and don't forget your legs."

3.10 »Ach, Vater.« sagte Hänsel,

"Oh, father." said Hansel,

3.11 »ich sehe nach meinem weißen Kätzchen,

"I'm looking after my white kitten,

3.12 das sitzt oben auf dem Dache und will mir Ade sagen.«

who is sitting on the roof and wants to say goodbye to me."

Die Frau sprach: 3.13
The woman said,

»Narr, das ist dein Kätzchen nicht, das ist die   3.14
Morgensonne, die auf den Schornstein scheint.«
"Fool, that's not your kitten, it's the morning sun shining
on the chimney."

Hänsel aber hatte nicht nach dem Kätzchen gesehen,   3.15
sondern immer einen von den blanken Kieselsteinen
aus seiner Tasche auf den Weg geworfen.
Hansel, however, had not looked at the kitten, but had
always thrown one of the shiny pebbles from his pocket
onto the path.

Als sie mitten in den Wald gekommen waren,   4.1
When they had reached the middle of the forest,

sprach der Vater: 4.2
the father said:

»Nun sammelt Holz, ihr Kinder, ich will ein Feuer   4.3
anmachen, damit ihr nicht friert.«
"Now gather some wood, you children, I will light a fire so
that you won't freeze."

Hänsel und Gretel trugen Reisig zusammen,   4.4
Hansel and Gretel gathered brushwood,

einen kleinen Berg hoch.   4.5
a small mountain high.

Das Reisig ward angezündet, und als die Flamme   4.6
recht hoch brannte, sagte die Frau:
The brushwood was lit, and when the flame was quite high,
the woman said,

4.7 »Nun legt euch ans Feuer, ihr Kinder, und ruht euch aus, wir gehen in den Wald und hauen Holz.

"Now lie down by the fire, you children, and rest, we'll go into the forest and cut wood.

4.8 Wenn wir fertig sind, kommen wir wieder und holen euch ab.«

When we've finished, we'll come back and fetch you."

5.1 Hänsel und Gretel saßen am Feuer, und als der Mittag kam, aß jedes sein Stücklein Brot.

Hansel and Gretel were sitting by the fire, and when midday came, they each ate a piece of bread.

5.2 Und weil sie die Schläge der Holzaxt hörten, so glaubten sie, ihr Vater wäre in der Nähe.

And because they heard the sound of the wooden axe, they thought their father was nearby.

5.3 Es war aber nicht die Holzaxt, es war ein Ast, den er an einen dürren Baum gebunden hatte und den der Wind hin und her schlug.

But it was not the wooden axe, it was a branch which he had tied to a dry tree and which the wind was beating to and fro.

5.4 Und als sie so lange gesessen hatten, fielen ihnen die Augen vor Müdigkeit zu, und sie schliefen fest ein.

And when they had been sitting there for so long, their eyes fell closed with tiredness and they fell fast asleep.

5.5 Als sie endlich erwachten, war es schon finstere Nacht.

When they finally woke up, it was already dark night.

5.6 Gretel fing an zu weinen und sprach,

Gretel began to cry and said,

»Wie sollen wir nun aus dem Walde kommen!«   5.7

"How shall we get out of the forest now!"

Hänsel aber tröstete sie: 5.8

But Hansel comforted her:

»Wart nur ein Weilchen, bis der Mond aufgegangen   5.9
ist, dann wollen wir den Weg schon finden.«

"Just wait a little while until the moon has risen, then we'll
find our way."

Und als der volle Mond aufgestiegen war, so nahm   5.10
Hänsel sein Schwesterchen an der Hand und ging
den Kieselsteinen nach, die schimmerten wie
neugeschlagene Batzen und zeigten ihnen den Weg.

And when the full moon had risen, Hansel took his little
sister by the hand and went after the pebbles, which
gleamed like new stones and showed them the way.

Sie gingen die ganze Nacht hindurch und kamen bei   5.11
anbrechendem Tage wieder zu ihres Vaters Haus.

They walked the whole night through, and at daybreak
came again to their father's house.

Sie klopften an die Thür, und als die Frau aufmachte   5.12
und sah, daß es Hänsel und Gretel war, sprach sie:

They knocked at the door, and when the woman opened it
and saw that it was Hansel and Gretel, she said,

»Ihr bösen Kinder, was habt ihr so lange im Walde   5.13
geschlafen, wir haben geglaubt, ihr wolltet gar nicht
wiederkommen.«

"You wicked children, why have you slept so long in the
forest, we thought you would not come back at all."

5.14 Der Vater aber freute sich, denn es war ihm zu
Herzen gegangen, daß er sie so allein zurückgelassen
hatte.
But the father was glad, for it had gone to his heart that he
had left them so alone.

6.1 Nicht lange danach war wieder Not in allen Ecken,
und die Kinder hörten wie die Mutter nachts im Bette
zu dem Vater sprach:
Not long afterwards, there was need in every corner again,
and the children heard their mother say to their father in
bed at night:

6.2 »Alles ist wieder aufgezehrt, wir haben noch einen
halben Laib Brot, hernach hat das Lied ein Ende.
"Everything has been used up again, we still have half a loaf
of bread, after that the song will end.

6.3 Die Kinder müssen fort, wir wollen sie tiefer in den
Wald hineinführen, damit sie den Weg nicht wieder
herausfinden;
The children must leave, we want to lead them deeper into
the forest so that they can't find their way out again;

6.4 es ist sonst keine Rettung für uns.«
otherwise there's no rescue for us."

6.5 Dem Mann fiel's schwer aufs Herz und er dachte:
The man's heart sank and he thought:

6.6 »Es wäre besser, wenn du den letzten Bissen mit
deinen Kindern teiltest.«
"It would be better if you shared the last bite with your
children."

Aber die Frau hörte auf nichts, was er sagte, schalt ihn und machte ihm Vorwürfe.   6.7

But the woman didn't listen to anything he said, scolded him and reproached him.

Wer A sagt, muß auch B sagen, und weil er das erste Mal nachgegeben hatte, so mußte er es auch zum zweitenmal.   6.8

He who says A, must also say B, and because he had given in the first time, he had to say it a second time.

Die Kinder waren aber noch wach gewesen und hatten das Gespräch mit angehört.   7.1

But the children were still awake and had overheard the conversation.

Als die Alten schliefen, stand Hänsel wieder auf, wollte hinaus und Kieselsteine auflesen, wie das vorige Mal, aber die Frau hatte die Thür verschlossen, und Hänsel konnte nicht heraus.   7.2

When the old people were asleep, Hansel got up again and wanted to go out and pick up pebbles, as he had done before, but the woman had locked the door and Hansel could not get out.

Aber er tröstete sein Schwesterchen und sprach: 7.3

But he comforted his little sister and said,

»Weine nicht, Gretel, und schlaf nur ruhig, der liebe Gott wird uns schon helfen.«   7.4

"Don't cry, Gretel, and sleep peacefully, the good Lord will help us."

Am frühen Morgen kam die Frau und holte die Kinder aus dem Bette.   8.1

Early in the morning, the woman came and got the children out of bed.

8.2 **Sie erhielten ihr Stückchen Brot,**
They were given their piece of bread,

8.3 **das war aber noch kleiner als das vorige Mal.**
but it was even smaller than the previous time.

8.4 **Auf dem Wege nach dem Walde bröckelte es Hänsel in der Tasche, stand oft still und warf ein Bröcklein, auf die Erde.**
On the way to the forest it crumbled in Hansel's pocket, he often stood still and threw a crumb on the ground.

8.5 **»Hänsel, was stehst du und guckst dich um.«**
"Hansel, why are you standing and looking around."

8.6 **sagte der Vater, »geh deiner Wege.«**
said his father, "go your way."

8.7 **»Ich sehe nach meinem Täubchen,**
"I'm looking after my little dove,

8.8 **das sitzt auf dem Dache und will mir Ade sagen.«**
she's sitting on the roof and wants to say goodbye to me."

8.9 **antwortete Hänsel. »Narr.« sagte die Frau,**
answered Hansel. "Fool." said the woman,

8.10 **»das ist dein Täubchen nicht, das ist die Morgensonne, die auf den Schornstein oben scheint.«**
"that's not your pigeon, it's the morning sun shining on the chimney above."

8.11 **Hänsel aber warf nach und nach alle Bröcklein auf den Weg.**
Hansel, however, threw all the crumbs one by one onto the path.

Die Frau führte die Kinder noch tiefer in den Wald,   9.1
The woman led the children even deeper into the forest,

wo sie ihr Lebtag noch nicht gewesen waren.   9.2
where they had never been before in their lives.

Da ward wieder ein großes Feuer angemacht, und die   9.3
Mutter sagte:
Then another big fire was lit, and the mother said,

»Bleibt nur da sitzen, ihr Kinder, und wenn ihr müde   9.4
seid, könnt ihr ein wenig schlafen;
"Just sit there, you children, and when you are tired you
can sleep a little;

wir gehen in den Wald und hauen Holz, und abends,   9.5
wenn wir fertig sind, kommen wir und holen euch
ab.«
we will go into the forest and cut wood, and in the evening,
when we have finished, we will come and fetch you."

Als es Mittag war, teilte Gretel ihr Brot mit Hänsel,   9.6
der sein Stück auf den Weg gestreut hatte.
When it was noon, Gretel shared her bread with Hansel,
who had scattered his piece on the path.

Dann schliefen sie ein, und der Abend verging, aber   9.7
niemand kam zu den armen Kindern.
Then they fell asleep and the evening passed, but no one
came to see the poor children.

Sie erwachten erst in der finsteren Nacht,   9.8
They only woke up in the dark night,

und Hänsel tröstete sein Schwesterchen und sagte: 9.9
and Hansel comforted his little sister and said:

9.10 »Wart nur, Gretel, bis der Mond aufgeht, dann
werden wir die Brotbröcklein sehen, die ich
ausgestreut habe, die zeigen uns den Weg nach
Hause.«

"Just wait, Gretel, until the moon rises, then we will see
the crumbs of bread that I have scattered, they will show us
the way home."

9.11 Als der Mond kam, machten sie sich auf, aber sie
fanden kein Bröcklein mehr, denn die viel tausend
Vögel, die im Walde und im Felde umherfliegen, die
hatten sie weggepickt.

When the moon came, they set out, but they found no
more crumbs, for the thousands of birds flying about in the
woods and fields had pecked them away.

9.12 Hänsel sagte zu Gretel: »Wir werden den Weg schon
finden.«

Hansel said to Gretel, "We will find the way."

9.13 aber sie fanden ihn nicht.

but they did not find it.

9.14 Sie gingen die ganze Nacht und noch einen Tag von
Morgen bis Abend, aber sie kamen aus dem Walde
nicht heraus, und waren so hungrig, denn sie hatten
nichts als die paar Beeren, die auf der Erde standen.

They walked all night and another day from morning till
evening, but they did not get out of the forest, and were so
hungry, for they had nothing but the few berries that stood
on the ground.

Und weil sie so müde waren, daß die Beine sie nicht mehr tragen wollten, so legten sie sich unter einen Baum und schliefen ein.

And because they were so tired that their legs would no longer carry them, they lay down under a tree and fell asleep.

Nun war's schon der dritte Morgen, daß sie ihres Vaters Haus verlassen hatten.

It was now the third morning since they had left their father's house.

Sie fingen wieder an zu gehen, aber sie gerieten immer tiefer in den Wald und wenn nicht bald Hilfe kam, so mußten sie verschmachten.

They began to walk again, but they got deeper and deeper into the forest, and if help did not come soon, they were bound to die of hunger.

Als es Mittag war, sahen sie ein schönes schneeweißes Vöglein auf einem Ast sitzen, das sang so schön, daß sie stehen blieben und ihm zuhörten.

When it was noon, they saw a beautiful snow-white bird sitting on a branch, and it sang so beautifully that they stopped and listened to it.

Und als es fertig war, schwang es seine Flügel und flog vor ihnen her, und sie gingen ihm nach, bis sie zu einem Häuschen gelangten, auf dessen Dach es sich setzte, und als sie ganz nahe herankamen, so sahen sie, daß das Häuslein aus Brot gebaut war und mit Kuchen gedeckt;

And when it had finished, it waved its wings and flew before them, and they followed it till they came to a little house, on the roof of which it perched, and when they came very near they saw that the little house was built of bread, and covered with cakes;

10.5 aber die Fenster waren von hellem Zucker.
but the windows were of light sugar.

10.6 »Da wollen wir uns dranmachen.« sprach Hänsel,
"Let us go to it." said Hansel,

10.7 »und eine gesegnete Mahlzeit halten.
"and have a blessed meal.

10.8 Ich will ein Stück vom Dach essen, Gretel, du kannst, vom Fenster essen, das schmeckt süß.«
I will eat a piece from the roof, Gretel, you can eat from the window, it tastes sweet."

10.9 Hänsel reichte in die Höhe und brach sich ein wenig vom Dach ab, um zu versuchen, wie es schmeckte, und Gretel stellte sich an die Scheiben und knupperte daran.
Hansel reached up and broke off a bit of the roof to try how it tasted, and Gretel stood by the window and nibbled at it.

10.10 Da rief eine feine Stimme aus der Stube heraus:
Then a fine voice called out from the parlor:

»Knupper, knupper, kneischen,

"Knupper, knupper, kneischen,

wer knuppert an meinem Häuschen?«

Who's sniffing at my little house?"

12.1 die Kinder antworteten:
the children replied:

»Der Wind, der Wind,

"The wind, the wind,

das himmlische Kind.«

the heavenly child."

und aßen weiter, ohne sich irre machen zu lassen. 14.1

and went on eating without letting themselves be misled.

Hänsel, dem das Dach sehr gut schmeckte, riß ein 14.2
großes Stück davon herunter, und Gretel stieß eine
ganze runde Fensterscheibe heraus, setzte sich nieder
und that sich wohl damit.

Hansel, who liked the roof very much, tore off a large piece
of it, and Gretel pushed out a whole round window-pane,
sat down and enjoyed it.

Da ging auf einmal die Thür auf und eine steinalte 14.3
Frau, die sich auf eine Krücke stützte, kam
herausgeschlichen.

Then all at once the door opened and an old woman came
creeping out, leaning on a crutch.

Hänsel und Gretel erschraken so gewaltig, daß sie 14.4
fallen ließen, was sie in den Händen hielten.

Hansel and Gretel were so frightened that they dropped
what they held in their hands.

Die Alte aber wackelte mit dem Kopfe und sprach, 14.5

But the old woman shook her head and said,

»Ei, ihr lieben Kinder, wer hat euch hierher gebracht? 14.6

"Oh, dear children, who has brought you here?

Kommt nur herein und bleibt bei mir, 14.7

Come in and stay with me,

es geschieht euch kein Leid.« 14.8

no harm will come to you."

Sie faßte beide an der Hand und führte sie in ihr 14.9
Häuschen.

She took them both by the hand and led them into her little
house.

14.10 Da ward gutes Essen aufgetragen, Milch und Pfannkuchen mit Zucker, Äpfel und Nüsse.

Good food was served, milk and pancakes with sugar, apples and nuts.

14.11 Hernach wurden zwei schöne Bettlein weiß gedeckt und Hänsel und Gretel legten sich hinein und meinten, sie wären im Himmel.

Then two beautiful little white beds were made up and Hansel and Gretel lay down in them and thought they were in heaven.

15.1 Die Alte hatte sich nur so freundlich angestellt, sie war aber eine böse Hexe, die den Kindern auflauerte, und hatte das Brothäuslein bloß gebaut, um sie herbeizulocken.

The old woman had behaved so kindly, but she was a wicked witch who lay in wait for the children and had only built the little bread house to lure them in.

15.2 Wenn eins in ihre Gewalt kam, so machte sie es tot, kochte es und aß es, und das war ihr ein Festtag.

When she got hold of one, she killed it, cooked it and ate it, and that was a feast for her.

15.3 Die Hexen haben rote Augen und können nicht weit sehen, aber sie haben eine feine Witterung, wie die Tiere, und merken's, wenn Menschen herankommen.

The witches have red eyes and cannot see far, but they have a keen sense of smell, like animals, and can tell when people are approaching.

15.4 Als Hänsel und Gretel in ihre Nähe kamen, da lachte sie boshaft und sprach höhnisch:

When Hansel and Gretel came near her, she laughed maliciously and said mockingly,

»Die habe ich, die sollen mir nicht wieder entwischen.«   15.5

"I've got them, and I won't let them get away again."

Früh morgens, ehe die Kinder erwacht waren, stand   15.6
sie schon auf, und als sie beide so lieblich ruhen sah,
mit den vollen roten Backen, so murmelte sie vor sich
hin,

Early in the morning, before the children were awake, she
got up, and when she saw them both resting so sweetly,
with their full red cheeks, she murmured to herself,

»Das wird ein guter Bissen werden.«   15.7

"That will be a good morsel."

Da packte sie Hänsel mit ihrer dürren Hand und trug   15.8
ihn in einen kleinen Stall und sperrte ihn mit einer
Gitterthür ein;

Then she seized Hansel with her thin hand, and carried him
into a little stable, and shut him in with a barred door;

er mochte schreien wie er wollte, es half ihm nichts.   15.9

he might cry as much as he liked, it was of no use to him.

Dann ging sie zur Gretel, rüttelte sie wach und rief: 15.10

Then she went to Gretel, shook her awake, and cried,

»Steh auf, Faulenzerin, trag Wasser und koch deinem   15.11
Bruder etwas Gutes, der sitzt draußen im Stall und
soll fett werden.

"Get up, sluggard, carry some water, and cook your brother
something good, for he is sitting out in the stable, and shall
grow fat.

Wenn er fett ist, so will ich ihn essen.«   15.12

When he is fat, I will eat him."

15.13 Gretel fing an bitterlich zu weinen, aber es war alles vergeblich, sie mußte thun, was die böse Hexe verlangte.

Gretel began to weep bitterly, but it was all in vain; she had to do as the wicked witch demanded.

16.1 Nun ward dem armen Hänsel das beste Essen gekocht,

Now the best food was cooked for poor Hansel,

16.2 aber Gretel bekam nichts als Krebsschalen.

but Gretel got nothing but crab shells.

16.3 Jeden Morgen schlich die Alte zu dem Ställchen und rief:

Every morning the old woman crept to the stable and called out,

16.4 »Hänsel, streck deine Finger heraus, damit ich fühle, ob du bald fett bist.«

"Hansel, stick out your fingers, so that I may feel whether you will soon be fat."

16.5 Hänsel streckte ihr aber ein Knöchlein heraus, und die Alte, die trübe Augen hatte, konnte es nicht sehen und meinte, es wären Hänsels Finger, und verwunderte sich, daß er gar nicht fett werden wollte.

But Hansel put out a little knuckle, and the old woman, who had dim eyes, could not see it, and thought it was Hansel's fingers, and was surprised that he did not want to get fat at all.

16.6 Als vier Wochen herum waren und Hänsel immer mager blieb,

When four weeks had gone by and Hansel was still thin,

da übernahm sie die Ungeduld und sie wollte nicht   16.7
länger warten.
she became impatient and did not want to wait any longer.

»Heda, Gretel.« rief sie dem Mädchen zu,   16.8
"Heda, Gretel." she called to the girl,

»sei flink und trag Wasser; Hänsel mag fett oder   16.9
mager sein,
"be quick and carry water; Hansel may be fat or skinny,

morgen will ich ihn schlachten und kochen.«   16.10
tomorrow I will slaughter and cook him. "

Ach, wie jammerte das arme Schwesterchen, als es   16.11
das Wasser tragen mußte, und wie flossen ihm die
Thränen über die Backen herunter!
Oh, how the poor little sister wailed when she had to carry
the water, and how the tears flowed down her cheeks!

»Lieber Gott, hilf uns doch.« rief sie aus,   16.12
"Dear God, help us." she exclaimed,

»hätten uns nur die wilden Tiere im Wald gefressen,   16.13
"if only the wild beasts in the forest had eaten us,

so wären wir doch zusammen gestorben.«   16.14
we would have died together."

»Spare nur dein Geplärre.« sagte die Alte,   16.15
"Don't go on blabbering." said the old woman,

»es hilft dir alles nichts.«   16.16
"it won't do you any good. "

Früh morgens mußte Gretel heraus,   17.1
Gretel had to go out early in the morning,

184

17.2 den Kessel mit Wasser aufhängen und Feuer anzünden.

hang up the kettle of water and light the fire.

17.3 »Erst wollen wir backen.« sagte die Alte,

"Let's bake first." said the old woman,

17.4 »ich habe den Backofen schon eingeheizt und den Teig geknetet!«

"I've already heated the oven and kneaded the dough!"

17.5 Sie stieß das arme Gretel hinaus zu dem Backofen,

She pushed poor Gretel out to the oven,

17.6 aus dem die Feuerflammen schon herausschlugen.

from which the flames were already leaping.

17.7 »Kriech hinein.« sagte die Hexe,

"Crawl in." said the witch,

17.8 »und sieh zu, ob schon recht eingeheizt ist, damit wir das Brot hineinschießen können.«

"and see if it's heated properly so that we can put the bread in."

17.9 Und wenn Gretel darin war, wollte sie den Ofen zumachen und Gretel sollte darin braten, und dann wollte sie's auch aufessen.

And when Gretel was inside, she wanted to close the oven and let Gretel fry in it, and then she wanted to eat it.

17.10 Aber Gretel merkte, was sie im Sinn hatte, und sprach,

But Gretel realized what she had in mind and said,

17.11 »Ich weiß nicht, wie ich's machen soll;

"I don't know how to do it;

wie komm ich da hinein?«   17.12
how can I get in there?"

»Dumme Gans.« sagte die Alte,   17.13
"Silly goose." said the old woman,

»die Öffnung ist groß genug, siehst du wohl, ich   17.14
könnte selbst hinein.«
"the opening is big enough, you see, I could get in myself."

krabbelte heran und steckte den Kopf in den   17.15
Backofen.
She crawled up and stuck her head into the oven.

Da gab ihr Gretel einen Stoß, daß sie weit hineinfuhr,   17.16
machte die eiserne Thür zu und schob den Riegel vor.
Then Gretel gave her a push so that she went far in, closed
the iron door, and pushed the latch forward.

Hu! da fing sie an zu heulen, ganz grauselig;   17.17
Then she began to howl, very horribly;

aber Gretel lief fort und die gottlose Hexe mußte   17.18
elendiglich verbrennen.
but Gretel ran away, and the wicked witch was left to burn
miserably.

Gretel aber lief schnurstracks zum Hänsel,   18.1
But Gretel ran straight to Hansel,

öffnete sein Ställchen und rief: 18.2
opened his cage and called out:

»Hänsel, wir sind erlöst, die alte Hexe ist tot!«   18.3
"Hansel, we are saved, the old witch is dead!"

18.4 Da sprang Hänsel heraus wie ein Vogel aus dem Käfig, wenn ihm die Thür aufgemacht wird.
Then Hansel jumped out like a bird from a cage when the door was opened for him.

18.5 Wie haben sie sich gefreut, sind sich um den Hals gefallen, sind herumgesprungen und haben sich geküßt!
How happy they were, they threw their arms around each other's necks, jumped around and kissed!

18.6 Und weil sie sich nicht mehr zu fürchten brauchten, so gingen sie in das Haus der Hexe hinein, da standen in allen Ecken Kasten mit Perlen und Edelsteinen.
And because they no longer needed to be afraid, they went into the witch's house, where there were boxes of pearls and precious stones in every corner.

18.7 »Die sind noch besser als Kieselsteine.«
"They are even better than pebbles."

18.8 sagte Hänsel und steckte in seine Taschen was hinein wollte, und Gretel sagte,
said Hansel, putting what he wanted into his pockets, and Gretel said,

18.9 »Ich will auch etwas mit nach Hause bringen.«
"I want to bring something home too."

18.10 und füllte sich sein Schürzchen voll.
and filled his little apron.

18.11 »Aber jetzt wollen wir fort.« sagte Hänsel,
"But now let's go." said Hansel,

18.12 »damit wir aus dem Hexenwalde herauskommen.«
"so that we can get out of the witches' forest."

Als sie aber ein paar Stunden gegangen waren,   18.13
But when they had walked for a few hours,

gelangten sie an ein großes Wasser.   18.14
they came to a large body of water.

»Wir können nicht hinüber.« sprach Hänsel,   18.15
"We can't cross over." said Hansel,

»ich sehe keinen Steg und keine Brücke.«   18.16
"I can't see any footbridge or bridge."

»Hier fährt auch kein Schiffchen.« antwortete Gretel,   18.17
"There's no boat here either." replied Gretel,

»aber da schwimmt eine weiße Ente, wenn ich die   18.18
bitte, so hilft sie uns hinüber.«
"but there's a white duck swimming, if I ask her, she'll help
us across."

Da rief sie: 18.19
Then she called out:

»Entchen, Entchen,	"Ducklings, ducklings,
da steht Gretel und Hänsel.	it says Gretel and Hansel.
Kein Steg und keine Brücke,	No footbridge and no bridge,
nimm uns auf deinen weißen Rücken.«	take us on your white back."

20.1 Das Entchen kam auch heran, und Hänsel setzte sich auf und bat sein Schwesterchen, sich zu ihm zu setzen.

The duckling came too, and Hansel sat up and asked his little sister to sit with him.

20.2 »Nein.« antwortete Gretel,

"No." answered Gretel,

20.3 »es wird dem Entchen zu schwer,

"it will be too hard for the duckling,

20.4 es soll uns nacheinander hinüberbringen.«

he shall take us over one by one."

20.5 Das that das gute Tierchen, und als sie glücklich drüben waren und ein Weilchen fortgingen, da kam ihnen der Wald immer bekannter und immer bekannter vor, und endlich erblickten sie von weitem ihres Vaters Haus.

The good little animal did so, and when they were happily over there and had walked on for a while, the forest seemed more and more familiar to them, and at last they saw their father's house from afar.

20.6 Da fingen sie an zu laufen,

Then they began to run,

20.7 stürzten in die Stube hinein und fielen ihrem Vater um den Hals.

rushed into the parlor and threw their arms around their father's neck.

20.8 Der Mann hatte keine frohe Stunde gehabt, seitdem er die Kinder im Walde gelassen hatte, die Frau aber war gestorben.

The man had not had a happy hour since he had left the children in the forest, but the woman had died.

Gretel schüttete sein Schürzchen aus, daß die Perlen und Edelsteine in der Stube herumsprangen, und Hänsel warf eine Handvoll nach der andern aus seiner Tasche dazu.   20.9

Gretel poured out his little apron so that the pearls and precious stones scattered about the room, and Hansel threw one handful after another out of his pocket.

Da hatten alle Sorgen ein Ende, und sie lebten in lauter Freude zusammen.   20.10

Then all their worries came to an end and they lived together in pure joy.

Mein Märchen ist aus, dort läuft eine Maus, wer sie fängt, darf sich eine große Pelzkappe daraus machen.   20.11

My fairy tale is over, there runs a mouse, whoever catches it can make a big fur hat out of it.

Die Rübe

The Turnip

1.1 **Es waren einmal zwei Brüder, die dienten beide als Soldaten, und war der eine reich, der andere arm.**
Once upon a time there were two brothers who both served as soldiers, one of whom was rich and the other poor.

1.2 **Da wollte der Arme sich aus seiner Not helfen,**
So the poor one wanted to help himself out of his misery,

1.3 **zog den Soldatenrock aus und ward ein Bauer.**
took off his soldier's coat and became a farmer.

1.4 **Also grub und hackte er sein Stückchen Acker und säte Rübsamen.**
So he dug and hoed his little plot of land and sowed turnip seed.

Der Same ging auf, und es wuchs da eine Rübe, die 1.5
ward groß und stark und zusehends dicker und
wollte gar nicht aufhören zu wachsen, sodaß sie eine
Fürstin aller Rüben heißen konnte, denn nimmer
war so eine gesehen, und wird auch nimmer wieder
gesehen werden.

The seed sprouted, and there grew a turnip, which grew
large and strong and thicker and thicker, and would not
stop growing, so that it could be called the princess of all
turnips, for never was such a turnip seen, nor will it ever be
seen again.

Zuletzt war sie so groß, daß sie allein einen ganzen 1.6
Wagen anfüllte, und zwei Ochsen daran ziehen
mußten, und der Bauer wußte nicht, was er damit
anfangen sollte, und ob's sein Glück oder sein
Unglück wäre.

At last it was so large that it alone filled a whole cart, and
two oxen had to pull it, and the farmer did not know what
to do with it, and whether it would be his fortune or his
misfortune.

Endlich dachte er: 1.7

At last he thought,

»Verkaufst du sie, was wirst du Großes dafür 1.8
bekommen, und willst du sie selber essen, so thun
die kleinen Rüben denselben Dienst;

"If you sell them, what great things will you get for them,
and if you want to eat them yourself, the little turnips will
do the same service;

am besten ist, du bringst sie dem König und machst 1.9
ihm eine Verehrung damit.«

the best thing is to take them to the King and worship him
with them."

1.10 Also lud er sie auf den Wagen, spannte zwei Ochsen vor, brachte sie an den Hof und schenkte sie dem König.

So he loaded them on the cart, harnessed two oxen, brought them to the court and gave them to the king.

1.11 »Was ist das für ein seltsam Ding?« sagte der König,

"What strange thing is this?" said the king,

1.12 »mir ist viel Wunderliches vor die Augen gekommen,

"I have seen many wonderful things,

1.13 aber so ein Ungetüm noch nicht;

but never such a monster;

1.14 aus was für Samen mag die gewachsen sein?

from what kind of seed might it have grown?

1.15 Oder dir gerät's allein und du bist ein Glückskind.«

Or it will come to you alone, and you will be a lucky child."

1.16 »Ach nein.« sagte der Bauer,

"Oh no." said the farmer,

1.17 »ein Glückskind bin ich nicht, ich bin ein armer Soldat, der, weil er sich nicht mehr nähren konnte, den Soldatenrock an den Nagel hing und das Land baute.

"I am not a lucky child, I am a poor soldier who, because he could no longer feed himself, hung up his soldier's coat and built the land.

1.18 Ich habe noch einen Bruder, der ist reich, und Euch, Herr König, auch wohl bekannt, ich aber, weil ich nichts habe, bin von aller Welt vergessen.«

I have another brother, who is rich, and well known to you, Mr. King, but I, because I have nothing, am forgotten by all the world."

Da empfand der König Mitleid mit ihm und sprach: 1.19

Then the king took pity on him and said,

»Deiner Armut sollst du überhoben und so von mir 1.20
beschenkt werden, daß du wohl deinem reichen
Bruder gleich kommst.«

"You shall be relieved of your poverty and receive such a
gift from me that you will be like your rich brother."

Da schenkte er ihm eine Menge Gold, Äcker, Wiesen 1.21
und Herden, und machte ihn steinreich, sodaß des
anderen Bruders Reichtum gar nicht konnte damit
verglichen werden.

So he gave him a lot of gold, fields, meadows and herds, and
made him so rich that the other brother's wealth could not
be compared with it.

Als dieser hörte, was sein Bruder mit einer einzigen 1.22
Rübe erworben hatte, beneidete er ihn und sann hin
und her wie er sich auch ein solches Glück zuwenden
könnte.

When he heard what his brother had acquired with a single
turnip, he envied him and pondered back and forth as to
how he could make such a fortune for himself.

Er wollt's aber noch viel gescheiter anfangen, nahm 1.23
Gold und Pferde und brachte sie dem König und
meinte nicht anders, der würde ihm ein viel größeres
Gegengeschenk machen, denn hätte sein Bruder
soviel für eine Rübe bekommen, was würde es ihm
für so schöne Dinge nicht alles tragen.

But he wanted to do it much more cleverly, took gold and
horses and brought them to the king, thinking that he
would give him a much greater gift in return, for if his
brother had received so much for a turnip, what would it
not cost him for such beautiful things.

1.24 Der König nahm das Geschenk und sagte:

The king took the gift and said,

1.25 »Er wüßte ihm nichts wieder zu geben, das seltener und besser wäre als die große Rübe.«

"He would not know what to give him in return that was rarer and better than the great turnip."

1.26 Also mußte der Reiche seines Bruders Rübe auf einen Wagen legen und nach Hause fahren lassen.

So the rich man had to put his brother's turnip on a cart and take it home.

1.27 Daheim wußte er nicht an wem er seinen Zorn und Ärger auslassen sollte, bis ihm böse Gedanken kamen, und er beschloß seinen Bruder zu töten.

At home, he didn't know who to take his anger and resentment out on, until evil thoughts came to him and he decided to kill his brother.

1.28 Er gewann Mörder, die mußten sich in einen Hinterhalt stellen, und darauf ging er zu seinem Bruder und sprach:

He got murderers, they had to set themselves up in an ambush, and then he went to his brother and said,

1.29 »Lieber Bruder, ich weiß, einen heimlichen Schatz, den wollen wir miteinander heben und teilen.«

"Dear brother, I know a secret treasure that we want to raise and share together."

1.30 Der andere ließ sich's auch gefallen und ging, ohne Arg mit.

The other also agreed and went along without argument.

Als sie aber hinaus kamen, stürzten die Mörder über   1.31
ihn her, banden ihn und wollten ihn an einen Baum
hängen.

But when they came out, the murderers rushed upon him,
tied him up and wanted to hang him from a tree.

Indem sie eben darüber waren, erscholl aus der   1.32
Ferne lauter Gesang und Hufschlag, daß ihnen der
Schrecken in den Leib fuhr und sie über Hals und
Kopf ihren Gefangenen in den Sack steckten, am Ast
hinaufwanden und die Flucht ergriffen.

Just as they were about to do so, they heard loud singing
and hoof-beats from afar, which struck terror into their
hearts, and they put their prisoner into the sack over his
neck and head, and then they went up the branch and fled.

Er aber arbeitete oben bis er ein Loch im Sack hatte,   1.33
wodurch er den Kopf stecken konnte.

But he worked at the top until he had a hole in the sack
through which he could put his head.

Wer aber des Weges, kam, war nichts als ein   1.34
fahrender Schüler, ein junger Geselle, der fröhlich
sein Lied singend durch den Wald auf der Straße
daher ritt.

But whoever came along the path was nothing but a
traveling apprentice, a young journeyman, who rode
merrily along the road through the forest singing his song.

Wie der oben nun merkte, daß einer unter ihm   1.35
vorbeiging, rief er:

When he noticed that someone was passing below him, he
called out:

»Sei mir gegrüßt zu guter Stunde.«   1.36

"Greetings at a good hour."

1.37 Der Schüler guckte sich überall um, wußte nicht, wo die Stimme herschallte, endlich sprach er:
The pupil looked all around him, not knowing where the voice came from, and at last he said,

1.38 »Wer ruft mich?« Da antwortete er aus dem Gipfel:
"Who is calling me?" Then he answered from the summit:

1.39 »Erhebe deine Augen, ich sitze hier oben im Sack der Weisheit;
"Lift up your eyes, I am sitting up here in the sack of wisdom;

1.40 in kurzer Zeit habe ich große Dinge gelernt,
in a short time I have learned great things,

1.41 dagegen sind alle Schulen ein Wind;
in comparison all schools are a wind;

1.42 um ein Weniges, so werde ich ausgelernt haben, herabsteigen und weiser sein als alle Menschen.
by a little, I will have learned, descend and be wiser than all men.

1.43 Ich verstehe die Gestirne und Himmelszeichen, das Wehen aller Winde, den Sand im Meer, Heilung der Krankheit, die Kräfte der Kräuter, Vögel und Steine.
I understand the stars and heavenly signs, the blowing of all winds, the sand in the sea, the healing of sickness, the powers of herbs, birds and stones.

1.44 Wärst du einmal darin, du würdest fühlen, was für Herrlichkeit aus dem Sack der Weisheit fließt.«
If you were in it once, you would feel what glory flows from the sack of wisdom."

Der Schüler, wie er das alles hörte, erstaunte und sprach: 1.45

The disciple, when he heard all this, was astonished and said:

»Gesegnet sei die Stunde, wo ich dich gefunden habe, könnt' ich nicht auch ein wenig in den Sack kommen?« 1.46

"Blessed be the hour when I found you, could I not come into the sack a little?"

Oben der antwortete, als thät er's nicht gerne: 1.47

He replied, as if he did not like to do so:

»Eine kleine Weile will ich dich wohl hinein lassen für Lohn und gute Worte, aber du mußt doch noch eine Stunde warten, es ist ein Stück übrig, das ich erst lernen muß.« 1.48

"I will let you in for a little while for your reward and good words, but you must wait another hour, there is a piece left which I must first learn."

Als der Schüler ein wenig gewartet hatte, war ihm die Zeit zu lang und er bat, daß er doch möchte hinein gelassen werden, sein Durst nach Weisheit wäre gar zu groß. 1.49

When the pupil had waited a little while, the time was too long for him and he asked to be let in, for his thirst for wisdom was too great.

Da stellte der sich oben, als gäbe er endlich nach und sprach: 1.50

So he stood up, as if finally giving in, and said,

1.51 »Damit ich aus dem Haus der Weisheit heraus kann,
mußt du den Sack am Strick herunterlassen, so sollst
du eingehen.«

"In order for me to leave the house of wisdom, you must let
down the sack by the rope, and then you shall enter."

1.52 Also ließ der Schüler ihn herunter, band den Sack auf
und befreite ihn, dann rief er selber,

So the pupil let him down, untied the sack and freed him,
then he himself called out,

1.53 »Nun zieh mich recht geschwind hinauf.«

"Now pull me up quickly."

1.54 und wollte geradstehend in den Sack einschreiten.
»Halt!«

and wanted to step straight into the sack. "Stop!"

1.55 sagte der andere, »so geht's nicht an.«

said the other, "that's no way to do it."

1.56 packte ihn beim Kopf, steckte ihn umgekehrt in den
Sack, schnürte zu und zog den Jünger der Weisheit
am Strick baumwärts, dann schwengelte er ihn in der
Luft und sprach,

He grabbed him by the head, put him upside down in the
sack, tied it up and pulled the disciple of wisdom up the
tree by the rope, then waved him in the air and said,

1.57 »Wie steht's, mein lieber Geselle?

"How are things, my dear fellow?

1.58 Siehe, schon fühlst du, daß dir die Weisheit kommt
und machst gute Erfahrung, sitze also fein ruhig, bis
du klüger wirst.«

See, you already feel that wisdom is coming to you and you
are gaining good experience, so sit still until you become
wiser."

Damit stieg er auf des Schülers Pferd, ritt fort,   1.59
schickte aber nach einer Stunde jemand, der ihn
wieder herablassen mußte.

With that he mounted his pupil's horse and rode away, but
after an hour he sent someone to lower him down again.

Das junggeglühte Männlein

The Young Annealed Man

1.1 Zur Zeit, da unser Herr noch auf Erden ging, kehrte er eines Abends mit dem heiligen Petrus bei einem Schmied ein und bekam willig Herberge.

At the time when our Lord was still walking on earth, he stopped one evening with St. Peter at a blacksmith's house and was willingly given shelter.

1.2 Nun geschah's, daß ein armer Bettelmann von Alter und Gebrechen hart gedrückt in dieses Haus kam und vom Schmied Almosen forderte.

Now it happened that a poor beggar, hard pressed by age and infirmity, came to this house and demanded alms from the blacksmith.

1.3 Des erbarmte sich Petrus und sprach:

Peter took pity on him and said,

1.4 »Herr und Meister, so dir's gefällt, heil ihm doch seine Plage, daß er sich selbst sein Brot möge gewinnen.«

"Lord and Master, if it pleases you, heal his affliction so that he may earn his own bread."

Sanftmütig sprach der Herr   1.5
The Lord meekly said,

»Schmied, leih mir deine Esse und lege mir Kohlen   1.6
an, so will ich den alten kranken Mann zu dieser Zeit
verjüngen.«
"Smith, lend me your forge and set me some coals, and I
will rejuvenate the old sick man at this time."

Der Schmied war ganz bereit, und St. Petrus zog die   1.7
Bälge, und als das Kohlenfeuer auffunkte, groß und
hoch, nahm unser Herr das alte Männlein, schob's in
die Esse, mitten ins rote Feuer, daß es drin glühte wie
ein Rosenstock und Gott lobte mit lauter Stimme.
The blacksmith was quite ready, and St. Peter drew the
bellows, and when the coal fire flared up, great and
high, our Lord took the old man, pushed him into the
furnace, right into the red fire, so that he glowed in it like a
rosebush, and praised God with a loud voice.

Nachdem trat der Herr zum Löschtrog, zog das   1.8
glühende Männlein hinein, daß das Wasser über
ihm zusammenschlug, und nachdem er's fein sittig
abgekühlt, gab er ihm seinen Segen;
Then the master stepped to the extinguishing-trough, drew
the glowing little man into it, so that the water beat over
him, and after he had cooled him down, he gave him his
blessing;

siehe, zuhand sprang das Männlein heraus, zart,   1.9
gerade, gesund und wie von zwanzig Jahren.
and behold, out sprang the little man, tender, straight,
healthy, and as if he were twenty years old.

Der Schmied, der eben und genau zugesehen hatte,   1.10
lud sie alle zum Nachtmahl.
The smith, who had just been watching closely, invited
them all to supper.

1.11 Er hatte aber eine alte halbblinde bucklige Schwieger, die machte sich zum Jüngling hin und forschte ernstlich, ob ihn das Feuer hart gebrannt habe.

But he had an old, half-blind, hunchbacked sister-in-law, who approached the young man and inquired earnestly whether the fire had burnt him hard.

1.12 Nie sei ihm besser gewesen, antwortete jener, er habe da in der Glut gesessen wie in einem kühlen Tau.

He had never been better, she replied, he had sat there in the embers like in a cool dew.

2.1 Was der Jüngling gesagt hatte, das klang die ganze Nacht in den Ohren der alten Frau, und als der Herr früh morgens die Straße weiter gezogen war und dem Schmied wohl gedankt hatte, meinte dieser, er könnte seine alte Schwieger auch jung machen, da er fein ordentlich alles mit angesehen habe und es in seine Kunst schlage.

What the young man had said rang in the old woman's ears all night long, and when the gentleman had moved on down the street early in the morning and thanked the blacksmith, he said he could make his old wife-in-law young, too, as he had seen everything so well and had put it into his art.

2.2 Rief sie deshalb an, ob sie auch wie ein Mägdlein von achtzehn Jahren in Sprüngen daher wollte gehen.

So he called her and asked her if she wanted to go in leaps and bounds like a girl of eighteen.

2.3 Sie sprach: »Von ganzem Herzen.«

She said, "With all my heart."

2.4 weil es dem Jüngling auch so sanft angekommen war.

because the young man had been so gentle.

Machte also der Schmied große Glut und stieß
die Alte hinein, die sich hin und wieder bog und
grausames Mordgeschrei anstimmte.

2.5

So the smith made a great blaze, and thrust the old woman
into it, who bent from time to time, and uttered cruel
murderous cries.

»Sitz still, was schreist und hüpfst du, ich will erst
weidlich zublasen.«

2.6

"Sit still, why are you screaming and jumping, I want to
blow hard first."

Zog damit die Bälge von neuem, bis ihr alle
Haderlumpen brannten.

2.7

She pulled the bellows anew until all her rags were on fire.

Das alte Weib schrie ohne Ruhe, und der Schmied
dachte,

2.8

The old woman screamed without rest, and the blacksmith
thought,

»Kunst geht nicht recht zu.«

2.9

"Art is not right."

nahm sie heraus und warf sie in den Löschtrog.

2.10

He took her out and threw her into the extinguishing
trough.

Da schrie sie ganz überlaut, daß es droben im Haus
die Schmiedin und ihre Schnur hörten;

2.11

Then she screamed so loudly that the blacksmith's wife and
her cord heard it in the house above;

2.12 die liefen beide die Stiegen herab, und sahen die Alte
heulend und maulend ganz zusammengeschnurrt
im Trog liegen, das Angesicht gerunzelt, gefaltet und
ungeschaffen.

they both ran down the stairs, and saw the old woman lying
in the trough, howling and mumbling, her face wrinkled,
folded, and unmade.

2.13 Darob sich die zwei, die beide mit Kindern gingen, so
entsetzten, daß sie noch dieselbe Nacht zwei Junge
gebaren, die waren nicht wie Menschen geschaffen,
sondern wie Affen, und liefen zum Wald hinein;

At this the two, who were both walking with children,
were so terrified that they gave birth that very night to
two young ones, who were not made like men, but like
monkeys, and ran into the forest;

2.14 und von ihnen stammt das Geschlecht der Affen her.

and from them came the race of monkeys.

Des Herrn und des Teufels Getier

The Lord's and the Devil's Beast

1.1 Gott der Herr hatte alle Tiere erschaffen und sich die Wölfe zu seinen Hunden auserwählet; bloß die Geiß hatte er vergessen.

The Lord God had created all the animals and had chosen the wolves to be his dogs, but he had forgotten the goats.

1.2 Da richtete sich der Teufel an, wollte auch schaffen und machte die Geißen mit feinen langen Schwänzen.

Then the devil set about creating them and made the goats with fine long tails.

1.3 Wenn sie nun zur Weide gingen, blieben sie gewöhnlich mit ihren Schwänzen in den Dornhecken hängen, da mußte der Teufel hineingehen und sie mit vieler Mühe losknüpfen.

Now when they went to pasture, they usually got their tails caught in the thorn hedges, so the devil had to go in and untie them with great difficulty.

Das verdroß ihn zuletzt, war her und biß jeder Geiß
den Schwanz ab, wie noch heutigen Tages an den
Stümpfen zu sehen ist.

This finally annoyed him and he came and bit off the tail of
every goat, as can still be seen from the stumps today.

Nun ließ er sie zwar allein werden, aber es geschah,
daß Gott der Herr zusah wie sie bald einen
fruchtbaren Baum benagten, bald die edeln Reben
beschädigten, bald andere zarte Pflanzen verdarben.

Now he left them alone, but it happened that the Lord
God saw how they sometimes devoured a fruitful tree,
sometimes damaged the noble vines, sometimes spoiled
other tender plants.

Das jammerte ihn, sodaß er aus Güte und Gnaden
seine Wölfe dran hetzte, welche die Geißen, die da
gingen, bald zerrissen.

This grieved him, so that out of kindness and mercy he sent
his wolves after them, which soon tore the goats to pieces.

Wie der Teufel das vernahm, trat er vor dem Herrn
und sprach,

When the devil heard this, he came before the Lord and
said,

»Dein Geschöpf hat mir das meine zerrissen.«

"Your creature has torn up my own."

Der Herr antwortete:

The Lord replied:

»Was hattest du es zum Schaden erschaffen!« Der
Teufel sagte,

"Why did you create it for harm!" The devil said,

2.7 »Ich mußte das;

"I had to;

2.8 gleichwie selbst mein Sinn auf Schaden geht, konnte was ich erschaffen keine andere Natur haben, und mußt mir's teuer zahlen.«

just as even my mind goes to harm, what I created could have no other nature, and you must pay me dearly for it."

2.9 »Ich zahl dir's, sobald das Eichenlaub abfällt, dann komm, dein Geld ist schon gezählt.«

"I will pay you as soon as the oak leaves fall off, then come, your money is already counted."

2.10 Als das Eichenlaub abgefallen war,

When the oak leaves had fallen off,

2.11 kam der Teufel und forderte seine Schuld. Der Herr aber sprach:

the devil came and demanded his debt. But the Lord said:

2.12 »In der Kirche zu Konstantinopel steht eine hohe Eiche,

"There is a tall oak tree in the church in Constantinople,

2.13 die hat noch alles ihr Laub.«

it still has all its leaves."

2.14 Mit Toben und Fluchen entwich der Teufel und wollte die Eiche suchen, irrte sechs Monate in der Wüstenei, ehe er sie fand, und als er wieder kam, waren derweil wieder alle anderen Eichen voll grüner Blätter.

With raving and cursing, the devil escaped and went in search of the oak, wandered for six months in the desert before he found it, and when he returned, all the other oaks were full of green leaves again.

Da mußte er seine Schuld fahren lassen, 2.15
Then he had to let go of his guilt,

stach im Zorn allen übrigen Geißen die Augen aus 2.16
und setzte ihnen seine eigenen ein.
and in anger he gouged out the eyes of all the other goats
and put in his own.

Darum haben alle Geißen Teufelsaugen und 3.1
abgebissene Schwänze,
That's why all goats have devil's eyes and bitten-off tails,

und er nimmt gern ihre Gestalt an. 3.2
and he likes to take their shape.

Der Hahnenbalken

The Cock Bar

1.1 Es war einmal ein Zauberer, der stand mitten in einer großen Menge Volks und vollbrachte seine Wunderdinge.

Once upon a time there was a magician who stood in the middle of a large crowd and performed miracles.

1.2 Da ließ er auch einen Hahn einherschreiten,

He had a rooster walk in,

1.3 der hob einen schweren Balken und trug ihn als wäre er federleicht.

which lifted a heavy beam and carried it as if it were as light as a feather.

1.4 Nun war aber ein Mädchen, das hatte eben ein vierblättriges Blatt gefunden und war dadurch klug geworden, sodaß kein Blendwerk vor ihm bestehen konnte, und sah, daß der Balken nichts war als ein Strohhalm.

Now there was a girl who had just found a four-leaved leaf, and had become wise enough to see that the beam was nothing but a straw.

Da rief es: 1.5
Then he cried,

»Ihr Leute, seht ihr nicht, das ist ein bloßer 1.6
Strohhalm und kein Balken, was der Hahn da trägt.«
"You people, do you not see that it is a mere straw, and not a
beam, which the cock is carrying."

Alsbald verschwand der Zauber, 1.7
Immediately the magic disappeared,

und die Leute sahen was es war und jagten den 1.8
Hexenmeister mit Schimpf und Schande fort.
and the people saw what it was and chased the sorcerer
away with shame and disgrace.

Er aber, voll innerlichen Zornes, sprach, 1.9
But he, full of inner anger, said,

»Ich will mich schon rächen.« 1.10
"I will take my revenge."

Nach einiger Zeit hielt das Mädchen Hochzeit, war 1.11
geputzt und ging in einem großen Zug über das Feld
nach dem Ort, wo die Kirche stand.
After some time, the girl had her wedding, was cleaned up
and went in a large procession across the field to the place
where the church stood.

Auf einmal kamen sie an einen stark 1.12
angeschwollenen Bach, und war keine Brücke und
kein Steg, darüber zu gehen.
Suddenly they came to a very swollen brook, and there was
no bridge or footbridge to cross it.

Da war die Braut flink, 1.13
The bride was quick,

1.14 hob ihre Kleider auf und wollte durchwaten.

picked up her clothes and wanted to wade through.

1.15 Wie sie nun eben im Wasser so steht, ruft ein Mann,
und das war der Zauberer, neben ihr ganz spöttisch:

As she was standing in the water, a man, and it was the
magician, called mockingly beside her,

1.16 »Ei! wo hast du deine Augen, daß du das für ein
Wasser hältst?«

"Why, where are your eyes, that you think this is water?"

1.17 Da gingen ihr die Augen auf und sie sah,

Then her eyes were opened,

1.18 daß sie mit ihren aufgehobenen Kleidern mitten in
einem blaublühenden Flachsfeld stand.

and she saw that she was standing in the middle of a field of
blue flax with her clothes on.

1.19 Da sahen es die Leute auch allesamt und jagten sie
mit Schimpf und Gelächter fort.

Then the people all saw it too, and chased her away with
scolding and laughter.

Die alte Bettelfrau

The Old Beggar Woman

1.1 **Es war einmal eine alte Frau,**
Once upon a time there was an old woman,

1.2 **du hast wohl ehe eine alte Frau sehn betteln gehn?**
have you ever seen an old woman begging?

1.3 **Diese Frau bettelte auch, und wenn sie etwas bekam, dann sagte sie:**
This woman also begged, and when she got something, she said:

1.4 **»Gott lohn Euch.«**
"God reward you."

1.5 **Die Bettelfrau kam an die Thür, da stand ein freundlicher Schelm von Jungen am Feuer und wärmte sich.**
The beggar woman came to the door, and there stood a friendly rascal of a boy by the fire, warming himself.

1.6 **Der Junge sagte freundlich zu der armen alten Frau, wie sie so an der Thür stand und zitterte,**
The boy said kindly to the poor old woman as she stood by the door, trembling,

»Kommt, Altmutter, und erwärmt Euch.« 1.7

"Come, old mother, and warm yourself."

Sie kam herzu, ging aber zu nahe ans Feuer stehn, 1.8
daß ihre alten Lumpen anfingen zu brennen und sie
ward's nicht gewahr.

She came over, but stood too near the fire, so that her old
rags began to burn, and she was not aware of it.

Der Junge stand und sah das, er hätt's doch löschen 1.9
sollen?

The boy stood and saw it, he should have put it out,
shouldn't he?

Nicht wahr, er hätte löschen sollen? 1.10

Shouldn't he have put it out?

Und wenn er kein Wasser gehabt hätte, dann hätte 1.11
er alles Wasser in seinem Leibe zu den Augen
herausweinen sollen, das hätte so zwei, hübsche
Bächlein gegeben zu löschen.

And if he had had no water, he should have cried out all
the water in his body to his eyes, that would have made two
pretty little streams to put out the fire.

Die drei Faulen

The Three Lazy Ones

1.1 Ein König hatte drei Söhne, die waren ihm alle gleich lieb, und er wußte nicht welchen er zum König nach seinem Tode bestimmen sollte.

A king had three sons, who were all equally dear to him, and he did not know which he should appoint king after his death.

1.2 Als die Zeit kam, daß er sterben wollte, rief er sie vor sein Bett und sprach:

When the time came for him to die, he called them to his bedside and said,

1.3 »Liebe Kinder, ich habe etwas bei mir bedacht, das will ich euch eröffnen:

"Dear children, I have thought of something I want to tell you:

1.4 welcher von euch der Faulste ist, der soll nach mir König werden.«

whichever of you is the laziest shall be king after me."

1.5 Da sprach der älteste:

Then the eldest said,

»Vater, so gehört das Reich mir, denn ich bin so faul,   1.6
wenn ich liege und will schlafen, und es fällt mir ein
Tropfen in die Augen, so mag ich sie nicht zuthun,
damit ich einschlafe.«

"Father, the kingdom is mine, for I am so lazy when I lie
down and want to sleep, and if a drop falls into my eyes, I
may not close them so that I fall asleep."

Der zweite sprach: »Vater, das Reich gehört mir,   1.7
denn ich bin so faul, wenn ich beim Feuer sitze
mich zu wärmen, so ließ ich mir eher die Fersen
verbrennen, eh' ich die Beine zurückzöge.«

The second said, "Father, the kingdom is mine, for I am
so lazy that when I sit by the fire to warm myself, I would
rather burn my heels than draw back my legs."

Der dritte sprach: »Vater, das Reich ist mein, denn   1.8
ich bin so faul, sollt ich aufgehängt werden und hätte
den Strick schon um den Hals, und einer gäbe mir
ein scharf Messer in die Hand, damit ich den Strick
zerschneiden dürfte, so ließ ich mich eher aufhängen,
eh' ich meine Hand erhübe zum Strick.«

The third said, "Father, the kingdom is mine, for I am so
lazy that if I were to be hanged and already had the rope
around my neck, and someone gave me a sharp knife in my
hand so that I could cut the rope, I would rather be hanged
than raise my hand to the rope."

Wie der Vater das hörte, sprach er,   1.9

When the father heard this, he said,

»Du hast es am weitesten gebracht und sollst der   1.10
König sein.«

"You have gone the furthest and shall be king."

Die zwölf faulen Knechte · 151 b. Die zwölf faulen Knechte

The Twelve Lazy Servants

1.1 Zwölf Knechte, die den ganzen Tag nichts gethan hatten, wollten sich am Abend nicht noch anstrengen, sondern legten sich ins Gras und rühmten sich ihrer Faulheit.
Twelve servants, who had done nothing all day, did not want to exert themselves in the evening, but lay down on the grass and boasted of their laziness.

1.2 Der erste sprach: »Was geht mich eure Faulheit an,
The first said, "What do I care about your laziness,

1.3 ich habe mit meiner eigenen zu thun.
I have my own to do.

1.4 Die Sorge für den Leib ist meine Hauptarbeit:
Taking care of my body is my main work:

1.5 ich esse nicht wenig und trinke desto mehr.
I eat not a little and drink all the more.

Wenn ich vier Mahlzeiten gehalten habe, so faste ich 1.6
eine kurze Zeit, bis ich wieder Hunger empfinde, das
bekommt mir am besten.
When I have had four meals, I fast for a short time until I
feel hungry again; that suits me best.

Früh aufstehen ist nicht meine Sache; 1.7
Getting up early is not my thing;

wenn es gegen Mittag geht, 1.8
if it is around noon,

so suche ich mir schon einen Ruheplatz aus. 1.9
I choose a place to rest.

Ruft der Herr, so thue ich, als hätte ich es nicht 1.10
gehört, und ruft er zum zweitenmal, so warte ich
noch eine Zeitlang, bis ich mich erhebe und gehe
auch dann recht langsam.
If the Lord calls, I act as if I hadn't heard him, and if he calls
a second time, I wait a while until I get up and even then I
walk quite slowly.

So läßt sich das Leben ertragen.« Der zweite sprach: 1.11
That is the way to bear life." The second said:

»Ich habe ein Pferd zu besorgen, aber ich lasse ihm 1.12
das Gebiß im Maul, und wenn ich nicht will, so
gebe ich ihm kein Futter und sage, es habe schon
gefressen.
"I have a horse to get, but I leave the bit in its mouth, and if
I don't want to, I don't give it any food and say it has already
eaten.

Dafür lege ich mich in den Haferkasten und schlafe 1.13
vier Stunden.
Instead, I lie down in the oat box and sleep for four hours.

1.14 Hernach strecke ich wohl einen Fuß heraus und fahre damit dem Pferd ein paarmal über den Leib, so ist es gestriegelt und geputzt;
After that, I stick out one foot and run it over the horse's body a few times, so it's groomed and cleaned;

1.15 wer wird da viel Umstände machen?
who's going to make a fuss?

1.16 Aber der Dienst ist mir doch noch zu beschwerlich.«
But the service is still too arduous for me."

1.17 Der dritte sprach: »Wozu sich mit Arbeit plagen?
The third said: "Why bother with work?

1.18 Dabei kommt nichts heraus.
Nothing will come of it.

1.19 Ich legte mich in die Sonne und schlief.
I lay down in the sun and slept.

1.20 Es fing an zu tröpfeln, aber weshalb aufstehen?
It started to drizzle, but why get up?

1.21 Ich ließ es in Gottes Namen fortregnen.
I let it rain away in God's name.

1.22 Zuletzt kam ein Platzregen und zwar so heftig, daß er mir die Haare vom Kopfe ausriß und wegschwemmte, und ich ein Loch in den Schädel bekam.
At last a downpour came, so heavy that it tore the hair from my head and washed it away, and I got a hole in my skull.

1.23 Ich legte ein Pflaster darauf und damit war's gut.
I put a plaster on it and that was that.

Schaden der Art habe ich schon mehr gehabt.« Der vierte sprach: 1.24

I have had more damage like that." The fourth said:

»Soll ich eine Arbeit angreifen, so dämmere ich erst eine Stunde herum, damit ich meine Kräfte spare.   1.25

"If I have to start work, I first doze around for an hour to save my strength.

Hernach fange ich ganz gemächlich an und frage, ob nicht andere da wären, die mir helfen könnten.   1.26

After that, I start at a leisurely pace and ask if there aren't others around who could help me.

Die lasse ich dann die Hauptarbeit thun,   1.27

Then I let them do the main work and just watch,

und sehe eigentlich nur zu; aber das ist mir auch noch zu viel.«   1.28

but that is still too much for me."

Der fünfte sprach: 1.29

The fifth said,

»Was will das sagen! Denkt euch, ich soll den Mist aus dem Pferdestall fortschaffen und auf den Wagen laden.   1.30

"What does that mean? Think of it as me taking the manure out of the stable and loading it onto the cart.

Ich lasse es langsam angehen, und habe ich etwas auf die Gabel genommen, so hebe ich es nur halb in die Höhe und ruhe erst eine Viertelstunde, bis ich es vollends hinaufwerfe.   1.31

I take it slowly, and when I have taken something on the fork, I only lift it halfway up and rest for a quarter of an hour before I throw it up completely.

1.32 Es ist übrig genug, wenn ich des Tags ein Fuder hinausfahre.

There's enough left over when I take a load out during the day.

1.33 Ich habe keine Lust mich tot zu arbeiten.« Der sechste sprach:

I have no desire to work myself to death." The sixth said,

1.34 »Schämt euch, ich erschrecke vor keiner Arbeit, aber ich lege mich drei Wochen hin und ziehe nicht einmal meine Kleider aus.

"Shame on me, I'm not afraid of any work, but I lie down for three weeks and don't even take off my clothes.

1.35 Wozu Schnallen an die Schuhe?

Why buckle my shoes?

1.36 Die können mir immerhin von den Füßen abfallen, es schadet nichts.

After all, they can fall off my feet, it won't do any harm.

1.37 Will ich eine Treppe ersteigen, so ziehe ich einen Fuß nach dem anderen langsam auf die erste Stufe herauf, dann zähle ich die übrigen, damit ich weiß, wo ich ruhen muß.«

If I want to climb a staircase, I slowly pull one foot after the other up to the first step, then I count the others so that I know where I have to rest."

1.38 Der siebente sprach: »Bei mir geht das nicht:

The seventh said: "That doesn't work for me:

1.39 mein Herr sieht auf meine Arbeit,

my master looks after my work,

1.40 nur ist er den ganzen Tag nicht zu Hause.

but he's not at home all day.

Doch versäume ich nichts, ich laufe soviel das
möglich ist, wenn man schleicht.

1.41

But I don't miss anything, I walk as much as I can, if you
sneak.

Soll ich fortkommen,

1.42

If I were to get away,

so müßten mich vier stämmige Männer mit allen
Kräften fortschieben.

1.43

four burly men would have to push me along with all their
strength.

Ich kam dahin, wo auf einer Pritsche sechs
nebeneinander lagen und schliefen:

1.44

I came to where six of them were lying next to each other
on a cot and sleeping:

ich legte mich zu ihnen und schlief auch.

1.45

I lay down with them and slept too.

Ich war nicht wieder zu wecken, und wollten sie
mich heim haben, so mußten sie mich wegtragen.«

1.46

I could not be woken up again, and if they wanted me home,
they had to carry me away."

Der achte sprach:

1.47

The eighth said,

1.48 »Ich sehe wohl, daß ich allein ein munterer Kerl bin, liegt ein Stein vor mir, so gebe ich mir nicht die Mühe, meine Beine aufzuheben und darüber hinweg zu schreiten, ich lege mich auf die Erde nieder, und bin ich naß, voll Kot und Schmutz, so bleibe ich liegen, bis mich die Sonne wieder ausgetrocknet hat:

"I see that I alone am a lively fellow; if there is a stone before me, I do not take the trouble to pick up my legs and walk over it, I lie down on the ground, and if I am wet, full of dung and dirt, I lie there until the sun has dried me out again:

1.49 höchstens drehe ich mich so, daß sie auf mich scheinen kann.«

at the most I turn round so that it can shine on me."

1.50 Der neunte sprach: »Das ist was Rechtes!

The ninth said, "That's right!

1.51 Heute lag das Brot vor mir, aber ich war zu faul, danach zu greifen, und wäre fast Hungers gestorben.

Today the bread lay before me, but I was too lazy to reach for it and nearly died of hunger.

1.52 Auch ein Krug stand dabei, aber so groß und schwer, daß ich ihn nicht in die Höhe heben mochte und lieber Durst litt.

There was also a jug, but it was so big and heavy that I didn't want to lift it up and preferred to suffer from thirst.

1.53 Mich nur umzudrehen, war mir zu viel, ich blieb den ganzen Tag liegen wie ein Stock.«

Just to turn around was too much for me, I lay there all day like a stick."

1.54 Der zehnte sprach: »Mir hat die Faulheit Schaden gebracht,

The tenth said: "Laziness brought me harm,

ein gebrochenes Bein und geschwollene Waden.

1.55

a broken leg and swollen calves.

Unser drei lagen auf einem Fahrweg und ich hatte die Beine ausgestreckt.

1.56

The three of us were lying on a road and I had my legs stretched out.

Da kam jemand mit einem Wagen und die Räder gingen mir darüber.

1.57

Someone came with a cart and the wheels went over me.

Ich hätte die Beine freilich zurückziehen können, aber ich hörte den Wagen nicht kommen:

1.58

I could have pulled my legs back, of course, but I did not hear the cart coming:

die Mücken summten mir um die Ohren,

1.59

the gnats buzzed around my ears,

krochen mir zur Nase hinein und zu dem Munde wieder heraus;

1.60

crawled in my nose and out my mouth again;

wer will sich die Mühe geben, das Geschmeiß weg zu jagen.«

1.61

who wants to take the trouble to chase away the mosquitoes."

Der elfte sprach: »Gestern habe ich meinen Dienst aufgesagt.

1.62

The eleventh said, "Yesterday I recited my service.

Ich hatte keine Lust, meinem Herrn die schweren Bücher noch länger herbei zu holen und wieder weg zu tragen:

1.63

I had no desire to fetch the heavy books for my master any longer and carry them away again:

1.64 **das nahm den ganzen Tag kein Ende.**
there was no end to it all day.

1.65 **Aber die Wahrheit zu sagen, er gab mir den Abschied und wollte mich auch nicht länger behalten, denn seine Kleider, die ich im Staube liegen ließ, waren von den Motten zerfressen;**
But to tell the truth, he bade me farewell and would not keep me any longer, for his clothes, which I had left in the dust, were eaten away by moths;

1.66 **und das war recht.« Der zwölfte sprach,**
and that was right." The twelfth said,

1.67 **»Heute mußte ich mit dem Wagen über Feld fahren,**
"Today I had to drive the cart across a field,

1.68 **ich machte mir ein Lager von Stroh darauf und schlief richtig ein.**
I made myself a bed of straw on it and fell fast asleep.

1.69 **Die Zügel rutschten mir aus der Hand, und als ich erwachte, hatte sich das Pferd beinahe losgerissen, das Geschirr war weg, das Ruckenseil, Kummet, Zaum und Gebiß.**
The reins slipped out of my hand, and when I awoke, the horse had almost broken loose, the harness was gone, the reins, bridle and bit.

1.70 **Es war einer vorbeigekommen, der hatte alles fortgetragen.**
Someone had come along and carried everything away.

1.71 **Dazu war der Wagen in eine Pfütze geraten und stand fest.**
The cart had also got into a puddle and was stuck.

Ich ließ ihn stehen und streckte mich wieder auf's Stroh.

1.72

I left it there and stretched out on the straw again.

Der Herr kam endlich selbst und schob den Wagen heraus, und wäre er nicht gekommen, so läge ich nicht hier, sondern dort und schliefe in guter Ruh.«

1.73

The master finally came himself and pushed the cart out, and if he hadn't come, I wouldn't be lying here, but there, sleeping in peace."

Das Hirtenbüblein

The Little Shepherd Boy

1.1 Es war einmal ein Hirtenbübchen, das war wegen
seiner weisen Antworten, die es auf alle Fragen gab,
weit und breit berühmt.

Once upon a time there was a little shepherd boy who was
famous far and wide for the wise answers he gave to all
questions.

1.2 Der König des Landes hörte auch davon,

The king of the country heard about it,

1.3 glaubte es nicht und ließ das Bübchen kommen.

didn't believe it and sent for the little boy.

1.4 Da sprach er zu ihm:

So he said to him:

1.5 »Kannst du mir auf drei Fragen, die ich dir vorlegen
will Antwort geben, so will ich dich ansehen wie
mein eigen Kind, und du sollst bei mir in meinem
königlichen Schloß wohnen.«

"If you can answer the three questions I put to you, I will
regard you as my own child and you shall live with me in
my royal castle."

Sprach das Büblein: »Wie lauten die drei Fragen?« 1.6

The little boy said, "What are the three questions?"

Der König sagte: »Die erste lautet: 1.7

The king said: "The first is:

Wie viel Tropfen Wasser sind in dem Weltmeer?« 1.8

How many drops of water are there in the ocean?"

Das Hirtenbüblein antwortete: 1.9

The little shepherd replied,

»Herr König, laßt alle Flüsse auf der Erde verstopfen, 1.10
damit kein Tröpflein mehr daraus ins Meer läuft, das
ich nicht erst gezählt habe, so will ich Euch sagen,
wie viel Tropfen im Meere sind.«

"Sir King, let all the rivers on earth be stopped up, so that
not a drop will run into the sea that I have not counted, and
I will tell you how many drops there are in the sea."

Sprach der König: »Die andere Frage lautet: 1.11

Said the king: "The other question is:

Wieviel Sterne stehen am Himmel?« Das 1.12
Hirtenbübchen sagte,

How many stars are there in the sky?" The little shepherd
said,

»Gebt mir einen großen Bogen weiß Papier.« 1.13

"Give me a large sheet of white paper."

1.14 und dann machte es mit der Feder so viel feine
Punkte darauf, daß sie kaum zu sehen und fast
gar nicht zu zählen waren und einem die Augen
vergingen, wenn man darauf blickte.

and then he made so many fine dots on it with his pen that
they could hardly be seen, and could hardly be counted,
and one's eyes grew dim when one looked at them.

1.15 Darauf sprach es:

Then he said,

1.16 »So viel Sterne stehen am Himmel als hier Punkte auf
dem Papier,

"There are as many stars in the sky as there are dots on this
paper,

1.17 zählt sie nur.« Aber niemand war dazu imstande.

just count them." But no one was able to do so.

1.18 Sprach der König: »Die dritte Frage lautet:

The king said: "The third question is:

1.19 Wie viel Sekunden hat die Ewigkeit?«

How many seconds does eternity have?"

1.20 Da sagte das Hirtenbüblein:

Then the little shepherd said:

1.21 »In Hinterpommern liegt der Demantberg, der hat
eine Stunde in der Höhe, eine Stunde in der Breite
und eine Stunde in der Tiefe;

"In the back of Pomerania lies the Demantberg, which
has one hour in height, one hour in width and one hour in
depth;

dahin kommt alle hundert Jahre ein Vögelein und 1.22
wetzt sein Schnäblein daran, und wenn der ganze
Berg abgewetzt ist, dann ist die erste Sekunde von der
Ewigkeit vorbei.«

a little bird comes there every hundred years and whets its
beak on it, and when the whole mountain is worn down,
then the first second of eternity is over."

Sprach der König: 2.1

Said the king:

»Du hast die drei Fragen aufgelöst wie ein Weiser und 2.2
sollst fortan bei mir in meinem königlichen Schlosse
wohnen,

"You have answered the three questions like a wise man
and shall henceforth live with me in my royal palace,

und ich will dich ansehen wie mein eigenes Kind.« 2.3

and I will regard you as my own child."

Die Sternthaler

The Sternthaler

1.1 Es war einmal ein kleines Mädchen, dem war Vater und Mutter gestorben, und es war so arm, daß es kein Kämmerchen hatte darin zu wohnen und kein Bettchen mehr darin zu schlafen und endlich gar nichts mehr als die Kleider auf dem Leib und ein Stückchen Brot in der Hand, das ihm ein mitleidiges Herz geschenkt hatte.

Once upon a time there was a little girl whose father and mother had died, and she was so poor that she had no room to live in, no bed to sleep in, and at last nothing but the clothes on her body and a piece of bread in her hand, which a compassionate heart had given her.

1.2 Es war aber gut und fromm.

But it was good and pious.

1.3 Und weil es so von aller Welt vergessen war, ging es im Vertrauen auf den lieben Gott hinaus in's Feld.

And because he was so forgotten by the world, he went out into the field, trusting in God.

1.4 Da begegnete ihm ein alter Mann, der sprach:

There he met an old man who said:

»Ach, gieb mir etwas zu essen, ich bin so hungrig.«   1.5
"Oh, give me something to eat, I'm so hungry."

Es reichte ihm das ganze Stückchen Brot und sagte,   1.6
He handed him the whole piece of bread and said,

»Gott segne dir's« und ging weiter.   1.7
"God bless you" and went on his way.

Da kam ein Kind, das jammerte und sprach: 1.8
Then came a child who was wailing and said:

»Es friert mich so an meinen Kopf, schenke mir   1.9
etwas, womit ich ihn bedecken kann.«
"My head is so cold, give me something to cover it with."

Da that es seine Mütze ab und gab sie ihm.   1.10
So he took off his cap and gave it to him.

Und als es noch eine Weile gegangen war, kam wieder   1.11
ein Kind und hatte kein Leibchen an und fror: da gab
es ihm seins;
And when he had gone a little while, another child came,
and had no tunic on, and was cold, so he gave him his;

und noch weiter, da bat eins um ein Röcklein, das gab   1.12
es auch von sich hin.
and still further on, another asked for a little skirt, which
he also gave him.

Endlich gelangte es in einen Wald, und es war schon   1.13
dunkel geworden, da kam noch eins und bat um ein
Hemdlein, und das fromme Mädchen dachte:
At last it came to a wood, and it was already dark, and
another came and asked for a shirt, and the pious girl
thought,

1.14 »Es ist dunkle Nacht, da sieht dich niemand, du kannst wohl dein Hemd weggeben.«

"It is dark night, no one can see you, you may as well give away your shirt."

1.15 und zog das Hemd ab und gab es auch noch hin.

and took off the shirt and gave it away too.

1.16 Und wie es so stand und gar nichts mehr hatte, fielen auf einmal die Sterne vom Himmel, und waren lauter harte blanke Thaler: und ob es gleich sein Hemdlein weggegeben, so hatte es ein neues an und das war vom allerfeinsten Linnen.

And as she stood there with nothing left, all at once the stars fell from the sky, and they were all hard, bright thalers, and though she had given away her shirt, she had a new one on, and it was of the finest linen.

1.17 Da sammelte es sich die Thaler hinein und war reich für sein Lebtag.

So he gathered the thalers into it, and was rich all his life.

Der gestohlene Heller

The Stolen Penny

1.1 Es saß einmal ein Vater mit seiner Frau und seinen Kindern mittags am Tisch, und ein guter Freund, der zum Besuch gekommen war, aß mit ihnen.

Once a father was sitting at the table at noon with his wife and children, and a good friend who had come to visit was eating with them.

1.2 Und wie sie so saßen und es zwölf Uhr schlug, da sah der Fremde die Thür aufgehen und ein schneeweiß gekleidetes, ganz blasses Kindlein hereinkommen.

And as they sat there and twelve o'clock struck, the stranger saw the door open and a snow-white, pale child come in.

1.3 Es blickte sich nicht um und sprach auch nichts,

It did not look around or speak,

1.4 sondern ging geradezu in die Kammer nebenan.

but went straight into the next room.

1.5 Bald darauf kam es zurück und ging ebenso still wieder zur Thür hinaus.

Soon afterwards it came back and went out of the door again just as quietly.

Am zweiten und am dritten Tage kam es auf eben diese Weise.   1.6

On the second and third day it came in the same way.

Da fragte endlich der Fremde den Vater, wem das schöne Kind gehörte, das alle Mittag in die Kammer ginge.   1.7

Then at last the stranger asked the father whose beautiful child it was that went into the chamber every noon.

»Ich habe es nicht gesehen.« antwortete er,   1.8

"I have not seen it." he replied,

»und wüßte auch nicht, wem es gehören könnte.«   1.9

"nor would I know to whom it could belong."

Am anderen Tage, wie es wieder kam, zeigte es der Fremde dem Vater, der sah es aber nicht, und die Mutter und die Kinder alle sahen auch nichts.   1.10

The next day, when it came back, the stranger showed it to the father, but he did not see it, and neither did the mother or the children.

Nun stand der Fremde auf, ging zur Kammerthür, öffnete sie ein wenig und ging hinein.   1.11

Now the stranger got up, went to the door of the chamber, opened it a little, and went in.

Da sah er das Kind auf der Erde sitzen und emsig mit den Fingern in den Dielenritzen graben und wühlen;   1.12

There he saw the child sitting on the ground, busily digging and rummaging with its fingers in the cracks of the floorboards;

wie es aber den Fremden bemerkte, verschwand es.   1.13

but when it noticed the stranger, it disappeared.

1.14 Nun erzählte er, was er gesehen hatte und beschrieb das Kind genau, da erkannte es die Mutter und sagte:

Now he told him what he had seen and described the child in detail, when the mother recognized him and said,

1.15 »Ach, das ist mein liebes Kind, das vor vier Wochen gestorben ist.«

"Oh, that's my dear child who died four weeks ago."

1.16 Sie brachen die Dielen auf und fanden zwei Heller, die hatte einmal das Kind von der Mutter erhalten, um sie einem armen Manne zu geben, es hatte aber gedacht,

They broke open the floorboards and found two pennies, which the child had once received from her mother to give to a poor man, but she had thought,

1.17 »Dafür kannst du dir einen Zwieback kaufen.«

"You can buy a rusk for that."

1.18 die Heller behalten und in die Dielenritzen versteckt: und da hatte es im Grabe keine Ruhe gehabt; und war alle Mittage gekommen, um nach den Hellern zu suchen.

She kept the pennies and hid them in the cracks of the floorboards, and there she had had no rest in the grave, and had come every day to look for the pennies.

1.19 Die Eltern gaben darauf das Geld einem Armen,

The parents then gave the money to a poor man,

1.20 und nachher ist das Kind nicht wieder gesehen worden.

and afterwards the child was not seen again.

Die Brautschau

The Bridal Show

1.1 Es war ein junger Hirt, der wollte gern heiraten und kannte drei Schwestern, davon war eine so schön wie die andere, daß ihm die Wahl schwer wurde und er sich nicht entschließen konnte, einer davon den Vorzug zu geben.

There was a young shepherd who wanted to marry and knew three sisters, one of whom was as beautiful as the other, so that it was difficult for him to choose and he could not make up his mind to give preference to one of them.

1.2 Da fragte er seine Mutter um Rat, die sprach:

So he asked his mother for advice, who said,

1.3 »Lade alle drei ein und setz ihnen Käs vor und hab acht wie sie ihn anschneiden.«

"Invite all three of them, and set cheese before them, and be careful how they cut it."

1.4 Das that der Jüngling;

The young man did so;

1.5 die erste aber verschlang den Käs mit der Rinde;

but the first devoured the cheese with the rind;

die zweite schnitt in der Hast die Rinde vom Käs ab,   1.6
weil sie aber so hastig war, ließ sie noch viel Gutes
daran und warf das mit weg;

the second cut the rind off the cheese in a hurry, but
because she was so hasty she left a lot of good stuff on it
and threw that away with it;

die dritte schälte ordentlich die Rinde ab,   1.7

the third peeled the rind off properly,

nicht zu viel und nicht zu wenig.   1.8

not too much and not too little.

Der Hirt erzählte das alles seiner Mutter, da sprach   1.9
sie,

The shepherd told all this to his mother, and she said,

»Nimm die dritte zu deiner Frau.«   1.10

"Take the third as your wife."

Das that er und lebte zufrieden und glücklich mit ihr.   1.11

So he did, and lived contentedly and happily with her.

Die Schlickerlinge

The Slips

1.1 Es war einmal ein Mädchen, das war schön, aber faul und nachlässig.

Once upon a time there was a girl who was beautiful, but lazy and careless.

1.2 Wenn es spinnen sollte, so war es verdrießlich, daß wenn ein kleiner Knoten im Flachs war, es gleich einen ganzen Haufen mit herausriß und neben sich zur Erde schlickerte.

When she had to spin, she was so annoyed that if there was a small knot in the flax, she immediately pulled out a whole heap of it and threw it to the ground beside her.

1.3 Nun hatte es ein Dienstmädchen, das war arbeitsam, suchte den weggeworfenen Flachs zusammen, reinigte ihn, spann ihn fein und ließ sich ein hübsches Kleid daraus weben.

Now she had a servant girl who was industrious, gathered the discarded flax, cleaned it, spun it finely and had a pretty dress woven from it.

Ein junger Mann hatte um das faule Mädchen geworben, und die Hochzeit sollte gehalten werden. 1.4
A young man had wooed the lazy girl and the wedding was to take place.

Auf dem Polterabend tanzte das fleißige Mädchen in seinem schönen Kleide lustig herum, 1.5
At the wedding feast,

da sprach die Braut: 1.6
the hard-working girl was dancing around in her beautiful dress when the bride spoke:

»Ach, wat kann dat Mäken springen   "Oh, what can dat girl jump

in minen Slickerlingen!«   in my slickers!"

Das hörte der Bräutigam und fragte die Braut, was sie damit sagen wollte. 3.1
The bridegroom heard this and asked the bride what she meant by it.

Da erzählte sie ihm, daß das Mädchen ein Kleid von dem Flachs trüge, den sie weggeworfen hätte. 3.2
She told him that the girl was wearing a dress made of the flax she had thrown away.

Wie der Bräutigam das hörte und ihre Faulheit bemerkte und den Fleiß des armen Mädchens, so ließ er sie stehen, ging zu jener und wählte sie zu seiner Frau. 3.3
When the bridegroom heard this and noticed her laziness and the poor girl's industriousness, he left her, went to her and chose her as his wife.

Der Sperling und seine vier Kinder

The Sparrow and its Four Children

1.1 Ein Sperling hatte vier Junge in einem Schwalbennest.

A sparrow had four young in a swallow's nest.

1.2 Wie sie nun flügge sind, stoßen böse Buben das Nest ein, sie kommen aber alle glücklich in Windbraus davon.

As they were fledging, bad boys broke into the nest, but they all escaped happily in a whirlwind.

1.3 Nun ist dem Alten leid, weil seine Söhne in die Welt kamen, daß er sie nicht vor allerlei Gefahr erst verwarnet und ihnen gute Lehren fürgesagt habe.

Now the old man is sorry because his sons came into the world, that he had not first warned them of all kinds of danger and told them good lessons.

2.1 Im Herbst kommen in einem Weizenacker viel Sperlinge zusammen;

In the fall, many sparrows come together in a wheat field;

allda trifft der Alte seine vier Jungen an,   2.2

there the old man meets his four young ones,

die führt er voll Freuden mit sich heim.   2.3

whom he takes home with him full of joy.

»Ach, meine lieben Söhne, was habt ihr mir den   2.4
Sommer über Sorge gemacht, dieweil ihr ohne meine
Lehre in Winde kamet;

"Oh, my dear sons, how you have troubled me all summer,
because you came to the winds without my teaching;

höret meine Worte und folget eurem Vater und sehet   2.5
euch wohl vor:

listen to my words and follow your father and beware:

kleine Vöglein haben große Gefährlichkeiten   2.6
auszustehen!«

little birds have great dangers to endure!"

Darauf fragte er den älteren, wo er sich den Sommer   2.7
über aufgehalten und wie er sich ernährt hätte.

He then asked the elder where he had spent the summer
and how he had fed himself.

»Ich habe mich in den Gärten gehalten, Räuplein und   2.8
Würmlein gesucht, bis die Kirschen reif wurden.«

"I stayed in the gardens, looking for caterpillars and worms
until the cherries were ripe."

»Ach, mein Sohn.« sagte der Vater,   2.9

"Ah, my son." said the father,

2.10 »die Schnabelweid ist nicht bös, aber es ist große Gefahr dabei, darum habe fortan deiner wohl acht, und sonderlich wenn Leute in Gärten umhergehen, die lange grüne Stangen tragen, die inwendig hohl sind und oben ein Löchlein haben.«

"the beak willow is not bad, but there is great danger in it, so be careful of you from now on, and especially when people walk around in gardens carrying long green sticks that are hollow inside and have a little hole in the top."

2.11 »Ja, mein Vater, wenn dann ein grün Blättlein aufs Löchlein mit Wachs geklebt wäre?«

"Yes, my father, if a little green leaf were stuck on the hole with wax?"

2.12 spricht der Sohn. »Wo hast du das gesehen?«

said the son. "Where did you see that?"

2.13 »In eines Kaufmanns Garten.« sagt der Junge. »O mein Sohn.«

"In a merchant's garden." said the boy. "O my son."

2.14 spricht der Vater, »Kaufleut, geschwinde Leut!

says the father, "merchants, swift folk!

2.15 bist du um die Weltkinder gewesen, so hast du Weltgeschmeidigkeit genug gelernt, siehe und brauch's nur recht wohl und trau dir nicht zu viel.«

if you have been about the children of the world, you have learned worldliness enough, see and use it well, and do not trust yourself too much."

3.1 Darauf befragt er den anderen:

He then asks the other:

3.2 »Wo hast du dein Wesen gehabt?«

"Where did you have your being?"

»Zu Hofe.« spricht der Sohn. 3.3

"At court." says the son.

»Sperling und alberne Vöglein dienen nicht an 3.4
diesem Ort, da viel Gold, Sammet, Seide, Wehr,
Harnisch, Sperber, Kautzen und Blaufüß sind, halt
dich zum Roßstall, da man den Hafer schwingt, oder
wo man drischet, so kann dir's Glück mit gutem Fried
auch dein täglich Körnlein bescheren.«

"Sparrows and silly little birds do not serve in this place,
where there is plenty of gold, velvet, silk, weir, armor,
sparrowhawks, chewing cows, and blue-sweet; keep to the
stable where the oats are swung, or where the threshing is
done, and good luck will bring you your daily grain with
good peace."

»Ja, Vater.« sagte dieser Sohn, 3.5

"Yes, father." said the son,

»wenn aber die Stalljungen Hebritzen machen und 3.6
ihre Maschen und Schlingen ins Stroh binden,

"but when the stable-boys make hay and tie their stitches
and snares in the straw,

da bleibt auch mancher behenken.« 3.7

some of them stay behind."

»Wo hast du das gesehen?« sagte der Alte. 3.8

"Where did you see that?" said the old man.

»Zu Hof, beim Roßbuben.« 3.9

"In the courtyard, with the knaves."

»O, mein Sohn, Hofbuben, böse Buben! 3.10

"O, my son, court-boys, bad boys!

248

3.11 bist du zu Hof und um die Herren gewesen und hast
keine Federn da gelassen, so hast du ziemlich gelernt
und wirst dich in der Welt wohl wissen auszureißen,
doch siehe dich um und auf;

If you have been at court and around the masters, and
have not left any feathers there, you have learned a good
deal, and will know how to get out in the world, but look
around you and up;

3.12 die Wölfe fressen auch oft die gescheiten Hündlein.«
the wolves often eat even the clever little dogs."

4.1 Der Vater nimmt den dritten auch vor sich:
The father also takes the third in front of him:

4.2 »Wo hast du dein Heil versucht?«
"Where did you try your luck?"

4.3 »Auf den Fahrwegen und Landstraßen hab ich Kübel
und Seil eingeworfen und da bisweilen ein Körnlein
oder Gräuplein angetroffen.«

"On the lanes and country roads I have thrown in buckets
and ropes, and sometimes I have come across a grain or a
little grass."

4.4 »Dies ist ja.« sagt der Vater,
"That's fine food." said the father,

4.5 »eine feine Nahrung, aber merk gleichwohl auf die
Schanz und siehe fleißig auf, sonderlich wenn sich
einer bücket und einen Stein aufheben will, da ist dir
nicht lang zu bleiben.«

"but watch your step and look out carefully, especially
when someone bends down and tries to pick up a stone."

4.6 »Wahr ist's.« sagt der Sohn,
"That's true." says the son,

»wenn aber einer zuvor einen Wand - oder Handstein   4.7
im Busen oder Tasche trüge?«

"but what if someone were carrying a stone in his bosom or
pocket first?"

»Wo hast du dies gesehen?«   4.8

"Where have you seen this?"

»Bei den Bergleuten, lieber Vater, wenn sie   4.9
ausfahren, führen sie gemeinlich Handsteine bei
sich.«

"With the miners, dear father, when they go out, they
usually carry handstones with them."

»Bergleut, Werkleut, anschlägige Leut!   4.10

"Miners, workmen, hard-working people!

bist du um Bergburschen gewesen,   4.11

If you have been around miners,

so hast du etwas gesehen und erfahren.   4.12

you have seen and experienced something.

Fahr hin und nimm deiner   Go there and take good
Sachen gleichwohl gut acht,   care of your things,

Bergbuben haben manchen   Mountain boys have
Sperling mit Kobold   killed many a sparrow
umbracht.«   with a goblin."

Endlich kommt der Vater an den jüngsten Sohn: 6.1

At last the father says to his youngest son,

6.2 »Du mein liebes Gackennestle, du warst allzeit der
albernste und schwächeste, bleib du bei mir, die
Welt hat viel grober und böser Vögel, die krumme
Schnäbel und lange Krallen haben und nur auf arme
Vöglein lauern und sie verschlucken;

"You, my dear little cluck, you have always been the silliest
and weakest, stay with me, the world has many coarse and
evil birds, which have crooked beaks and long claws and
only lie in wait for poor little birds and swallow them up;

6.3 halt dich zu deinesgleichen und lies die Spinnlein
und Räuplein von den Bäumen oder Häuslein,

stick to your own kind and pick the spiders and caterpillars
from the trees or little houses,

6.4 so bleibst du lang zufrieden.«

so you will stay happy for a long time."

6.5 »Du, mein lieber Vater, wer sich nährt ohne anderer
Leut Schaden, der kommt lang hin, und kein Sperber,
Habicht, Aar oder Weih wird ihm nicht schaden,
wenn er zumal sich und seine ehrliche Nahrung dem
lieben Gott all Abend und Morgen treulich befiehlt,
welcher aller Wald - und Dorfvöglein Schöpfer und
Erhalter ist, der auch der jungen Räblein Geschrei
und Gebet höret, denn ohne seinen Willen fällt auch
kein Sperling oder Schneekünglein auf die Erde.«

"You, my dear father, whoever feeds himself without
harming other people will get by for a long time, and no
sparrowhawk, goshawk, eagle or harrier will harm him,
especially if he faithfully commands himself and his honest
food to the dear God every evening and morning, who is
the creator and sustainer of all forest and village birds,
who also hears the cries and prayers of the young rabbits,
for without his will no sparrow or snowflake falls to the
ground."

»Wo hast du das gelernt?« Antwortet der Sohn: 6.6

"Where did you learn that?" Answered the son:

»Wie mich der große Windbraus von dir wegriß, 6.7
kam ich in eine Kirche, da las ich den Sommer die
Fliegen und Spinnen von den Fenstern ab und hörte
diese Sprüche predigen, da hat mich der Vater aller
Sperlinge den Sommer über ernährt und behütet vor
allem Unglück und grimmigen Vögeln.«

"When the great wind tore me away from you, I came
to a church, where I read the flies and spiders from the
windows during the summer and heard these sayings
preached, where the father of all sparrows fed me
throughout the summer and protected me from all
misfortune and fierce birds."

»Traun! mein lieber Sohn, fleuchst du in die Kirchen 6.8
und hilfest Spinnen und die sumsenden Fliegen
aufräumen und zirpst zu Gott wie die jungen Räblein
und befiehlst dich dem ewigen Schöpfer, so wirst du
wohl bleiben und wenn die ganze Welt voll wilder
tückischer Vögel wäre.

"My dear son, if you dart into the churches and help spiders
and buzzing flies to clean up, and chirp to God like the
young rabbits, and if you give yourself to the eternal
Creator, you will remain well, even if the whole world
were full of wild, treacherous birds.

Denn wer dem Herrn befiehlt seine Sach,	For he who commands the Lord his things,
schweigt, leidet, wartet, betet, braucht Glimpf, thut gemach,	is silent, suffers, waits, prays, needs comfort, does good,
bewahrt Glaub und gut Gewissen rein,	keeps faith and good conscience pure,

dem will Gott Schutz und
Helfer sein.«

to whom God wants to be
a protector and helper."

Das Märchen vom Schlauraffenland

The Fairy Tale of the Land of the Sly Monkeys

1.1 In der Schlauraffenzeit da ging ich, und sah an einem
kleinen Seidenfaden hing Rom und der Lateran,
und ein fußloser Mann der überlief ein schnelles
Pferd und ein bitterscharfes Schwert durchhieb eine
Brücke.

In the time of the sleeping monkeys I went and saw Rome
and the Lateran hanging on a small silk thread, and a
footless man who ran over a swift horse and a bitterly sharp
sword cut through a bridge.

1.2 Da sah ich einen jungen Esel mit einer silbernen Nase,
der jagte hinter zwei schnellen Hasen her, und eine
Linde, die war breit, auf der wuchsen heiße Fladen.

Then I saw a young donkey with a silver nose chasing
after two swift hares, and a broad lime tree with hot cakes
growing on it.

1.3 Da sah ich eine alte dürre Geiß, die trug wohl
hundert Fuder Schmalzes an ihrem Leibe und sechzig
Fuder Salzes.

Then I saw an old scrawny goat carrying a hundred
cartloads of lard and sixty cartloads of salt.

Ist das nicht gelogen genug?　　1.4
Is that not a lie enough?

Da sah ich ackern einen Pflug ohne Roß und Rinder,　　1.5
und ein jähriges Kind warf vier Mühlensteine von
Regensburg bis nach Trier und von Trier hinein
in Straßburg, und ein Habicht schwamm über den
Rhein:
Then I saw a plow plowing without horses and cattle, and
a year-old child threw four millstones from Regensburg
to Trier and from Trier into Strasbourg, and a hawk swam
across the Rhine:

das that er mit vollem Recht.　　1.6
he did that with full right.

Da hört ich Fische miteinander Lärm anfangen, daß　　1.7
es in den Himmel hinauf scholl, und ein süßer Honig
floß wie Wasser von einem tiefen Thal auf einen
hohen Berg;
Then I heard fishes making a noise together that made the
sky resound, and a sweet honey flowed like water from a
deep valley to a high mountain;

das waren seltsame Geschichten.　　1.8
these were strange stories.

Da waren zwei Krähen, mähten eine Wiese, und　　1.9
ich sah zwei Mücken an einer Brücke bauen, und
zwei Tauben zerrupften einen Wolf, zwei Kinder die
warfen zwei Zicklein, aber zwei Frösche droschen
miteinander Getreide aus.
There were two crows mowing a meadow, and I saw two
gnats building a bridge, and two pigeons tearing up a wolf,
two children throwing two kids, and two frogs threshing
grain together.

1.10 Da sah ich zwei Mäuse einen Bischof weihen, zwei Katzen, die einem Bären die Zunge auskratzten.

Then I saw two mice consecrating a bishop, two cats scratching out a bear's tongue.

1.11 Da kam eine Schnecke gerannt und erschlug zwei wilde Löwen.

Then a snail came running and killed two wild lions.

1.12 Da stand ein Bartscherer, schor einer Frau ihren Bart ab, und zwei säugende Kinder hießen ihrer Mutter stillschweigen.

There stood a beard shearer, shaving off a woman's beard, and two suckling children kept their mother quiet.

1.13 Da sah ich zwei Windhunde, brachten eine Mühle aus dem Wasser getragen, und eine alte Schindmähre stand dabei, die sprach, es wäre recht.

Then I saw two greyhounds carrying a mill out of the water, and an old shindy stood by, saying it was right.

1.14 Und im Hof standen vier Rosse, die droschen Korn aus allen Kräften, und zwei Ziegen, die den Ofen heizten, und eine rote Kuh schoß das Brot in den Ofen.

And in the yard stood four horses, threshing grain with all their might, and two goats heating the oven, and a red cow was putting bread into the oven.

1.15 Da krähte ein Huhn:

Then a hen crowed:

1.16 »Kikeriki, das Märchen ist auserzählt, kikeriki.«

"Cock-a-doodle-doo, the fairy tale is over, cock-a-doodle-doo."

Das Dietmarsische Lügenmärchen

The Dietmarian Tale of Lies

1.1 **Ich will euch etwas erzählen.**
Let me tell you something.

1.2 **Ich sah zwei gebratene Hühner fliegen, flogen schnell und hatten die Bäuche gen Himmel gekehrt, die Rücken nach der Hölle, und ein Amboß und ein Mühlstein schwammen über den Rhein, fein langsam und leise und ein Frosch saß und fraß eine Pflugschar zu Pfingsten auf dem Eis.**
I saw two roast chickens flying fast, with their bellies turned to heaven and their backs to hell, and an anvil and a millstone were floating across the Rhine, slowly and quietly, and a frog was sitting and eating a plowshare on the ice at Pentecost.

1.3 **Da waren drei Kerle, wollten einen Hasen fangen, gingen auf Krücken und Stelzen, der eine war taub, der zweite blind, der dritte stumm und der vierte konnte keinen Fuß rühren.**
There were three guys trying to catch a hare, walking on crutches and stilts, one was deaf, the second blind, the third dumb and the fourth couldn't move a foot.

259

Wollt ihr wissen, wie das geschah? 1.4

Do you want to know how this happened?

Der Blinde der sah zuerst den Hasen über das Feld 1.5
traben, der Stumme rief dem Lahmen zu, und der
Lahme faßte ihn beim Kragen.

The blind man first saw the hare trotting across the field,
the dumb man called to the lame man, and the lame man
took him by the collar.

Etliche die wollten zu Land segeln und spannten die 1.6
Segel im Wind und schifften über große Äcker hin:
da segelten sie über einen hohen Berg, da mußten sie
elendig ersaufen.

Some who wanted to sail on land stretched their sails in
the wind and sailed over large fields; then they sailed over a
high mountain and drowned miserably.

Ein Krebs jagte einen Hasen in die Flucht, und hoch 1.7
auf dem Dache lag eine Kuh, die war hinaufgestiegen.

A crab chased a hare into flight, and high on the roof lay a
cow that had climbed up.

In dem Lande sind die Fliegen so groß wie Ziegen. 1.8

In that country the flies are as big as goats.

Mache das Fenster auf, damit die Lügen 1.9
hinausfliegen.

Open the window and the lies will fly out.

260

Rätselmärchen

Riddle Tales

1.1 **Drei Frauen waren verwandelt in Blumen, die auf dem Felde standen, doch deren eine durfte des Nachts in ihrem Hause sein.**

Three women were changed into flowers that stood in the field, but one of them was allowed to be in her house at night.

1.2 **Da sprach sie auf eine Zeit zu ihrem Mann, als sich der Tag nahete und sie wiederum zu ihren Gespielen auf das Feld gehen und eine Blume werden mußte:**

Then she said to her husband at a time when the day was drawing near and she had to go again to her playmates in the field and become a flower:

1.3 **»So du heute vormittag kommst und mich abbrichst,**

"If you come this morning and break me off,

1.4 **werde ich erlöst und fürder bei dir bleiben.«**

I shall be delivered and remain with you for ever."

1.5 **was dann auch geschah.**

Which then happened.

Nun ist die Frage, wie sie ihr Mann erkannt habe, 1.6
so die Blumen ganz gleich und ohne Unterschied
waren?

Now the question is, how did her husband recognize her, if
the flowers were all alike and without distinction?

Antwort: 1.7

Answer:

»Dieweil sie die Nacht in ihrem Hause und nicht auf 1.8
dem Felde war, fiel der Tau nicht auf sie als auf die
anderen zwei, dabei sie der Mann erkannte.«

"Because she spent the night in her house and not in the
field, the dew did not fall on her as it did on the other two,
so that her husband recognized her."

Jungfrau Maleen

Maiden Maleen

1.1 **Es war einmal ein König, der hatte einen Sohn, der warb um die Tochter eines mächtigen Königs, die hieß Jungfrau Maleen und war wunderschön.**
Once upon a time there was a king who had a son who wooed the daughter of a powerful king, whose name was Maid Maleen and who was beautiful.

1.2 **Weil ihr Vater sie einem anderen geben wollte,**
Because her father wanted to give her to someone else,

1.3 **so ward sie ihm versagt.**
he was denied her.

1.4 **Da sich aber beide von Herzen liebten, so wollten sie nicht voneinander lassen, und die Jungfrau Maleen sprach zu ihrem Vater:**
But as they loved each other dearly, they would not leave each other, and the maiden Maleen said to her father,

1.5 **»Ich kann und will keinen anderen zu meinem Gemahl nehmen.«**
"I cannot and will not take anyone else as my husband."

Da geriet der Vater in Zorn und ließ einen finsteren Turm bauen, 1.6
Then the father became angry and had a dark tower built,

in den kein Strahl von Sonne oder Mond fiel. Als er fertig war, 1.7
into which no ray of sun or moon fell. When it was finished,

sprach er: 1.8
he said:

»Darin sollst du sieben Jahre lang sitzen, dann will ich kommen und sehen, ob dein trotziger Sinn gebrochen ist.« 1.9
"You shall sit in it for seven years, then I will come and see if your defiant spirit has been broken."

Für die sieben Jahre ward Speise und Trank in den Turm getragen, 1.10
Food and drink were carried into the tower for the seven years,

dann ward sie und ihre Kammerjungfer hineingeführt und eingemauert und also von Himmel und Erde geschieden. 1.11
then she and her chambermaid were led in and walled up and thus separated from heaven and earth.

Da saßen sie in der Finsternis, wußten nicht, wann Tag oder Nacht anbrach. 1.12
There they sat in darkness, not knowing when day or night came.

Der Königssohn ging oft um den Turm herum und rief ihren Namen, 1.13
The king's son often walked around the tower and called her name,

1.14 aber kein Laut drang von außen durch die dicken Mauern.

but no sound penetrated the thick walls from outside.

1.15 Was konnten sie anders thun als jammern und klagen?

What else could they do but moan and complain?

1.16 Indessen ging die Zeit dahin, und an der Abnahme von Speise und Trank merkten sie, daß die sieben Jahre ihrem Ende sich näherten.

Meanwhile, time went by, and they realized that the seven years were drawing to a close as their food and drink dwindled.

1.17 Sie dachten, der Augenblick ihrer Erlösung wäre gekommen, aber kein Hammerschlag ließ sich hören und kein Stein wollte aus der Mauer fallen:

They thought that the moment of their salvation had come, but no hammer was heard and no stone would fall from the wall:

1.18 es schien, als ob ihr Vater sie vergessen hätte.

it seemed as if their father had forgotten them.

1.19 Als sie nur noch für kurze Zeit Nahrung hatten und einen jämmerlichen Tod voraussahen,

When they only had food for a short time and were facing a miserable death,

1.20 da sprach die Jungfrau Maleen:

the maiden Maleen said:

1.21 »Wir müssen das letzte versuchen und sehen, ob wir die Mauer durchbrechen.«

"We must try one last thing and see if we can break through the wall."

Sie nahm das Brotmesser, grub und bohrte an dem Mörtel eines Steins, und wenn sie müde war, so löste sie die Kammerjungfer ab. 1.22

She took the bread knife, dug and drilled at the mortar of a stone, and when she was tired, she relieved the chambermaid.

Nach langer Arbeit gelang es ihnen, einen Stein herauszunehmen, dann einen zweiten und dritten, und nach drei Tagen fiel der erste Lichtstrahl in ihre Dunkelheit, und endlich war die Öffnung so groß, daß sie hinausschauen konnten. 1.23

After much labor they succeeded in taking out a stone, then a second and a third, and after three days the first ray of light fell into their darkness, and at last the opening was so large that they could look out.

Der Himmel war blau und eine frische Luft wehte ihnen entgegen, 1.24

The sky was blue and a fresh breeze blew towards them,

aber wie traurig sah ringsumher alles aus: 1.25

but how sad everything looked all around them:

das Schloß ihres Vaters lag in Trümmern, die Stadt und die Dörfer waren, so weit man sehen konnte, verbrannt, die Felder weit und breit verheert: 1.26

their father's castle lay in ruins, the town and villages were burnt as far as they could see, the fields were devastated far and wide:

keine Menschenseele ließ sich erblicken. 1.27

not a soul could be seen.

1.28 **Als die Öffnung in der Mauer so groß war, daß sie hindurchschlüpfen konnten, so sprang zuerst die Kammerjungfer herab, und dann folgte die Jungfrau Maleen.**

When the opening in the wall was large enough for them to slip through, the chambermaid jumped down first, followed by the maiden Maleen.

1.29 **Aber wo sollten sie sich hinwenden?**

But where should they go?

1.30 **Die Feinde hatten das ganze Reich verwüstet,**

The enemies had devastated the whole kingdom,

1.31 **den König verjagt und alle Einwohner erschlagen.**

chased away the king and slain all the inhabitants.

1.32 **Sie wanderten fort, um ein anderes Land zu suchen, aber sie fanden nirgend ein Obdach oder einen Menschen, der ihnen einen Bissen Brot gab, und ihre Not war so groß, daß sie ihren Hunger an einem Brennesselstrauch stillen mußten.**

They wandered off in search of another country, but they found no shelter or anyone who would give them a morsel of bread, and their need was so great that they had to satisfy their hunger on a stinging nettle bush.

1.33 **Als sie nach langer Wanderung in ein anderes Land kamen, boten sie überall ihre Dienste an, aber wo sie anklopften, wurden sie abgewiesen, und niemand wollte sich ihrer erbarmen.**

When, after a long journey, they came to another country, they offered their services everywhere, but wherever they knocked they were refused, and no one would have mercy on them.

Endlich gelangten sie in eine große Stadt, und gingen nach dem königlichen Hof. 1.34

At last they arrived in a large city and went to the royal court.

Aber auch da hieß man sie weiter gehen, bis endlich der Koch sagte, sie könnten in der Küche bleiben und als Aschenputtel dienen. 1.35

But even there they were told to go further, until finally the cook said they could stay in the kitchen and serve as Cinderella.

Der Sohn des Königs, in dessen Reich sie sich befanden, war aber gerade der Verlobte der Jungfrau Maleen gewesen. 2.1

But the son of the king, in whose kingdom they were, had just been the betrothed of the maiden Maleen.

Der Vater hatte ihm eine andere Braut bestimmt, 2.2

His father had chosen another bride for him,

die ebenso häßlich von Angesicht als bös von Herzen war. 2.3

who was as ugly in appearance as she was evil at heart.

Die Hochzeit war festgesetzt und die Braut schon angelangt; 2.4

The wedding was fixed, and the bride had already arrived;

bei ihrer großen Häßlichkeit aber ließ sie sich vor niemand sehen und schloß sich in ihre Kammer ein, und die Jungfrau Maleen mußte ihr das Essen aus der Küche bringen. 2.5

but in her great ugliness she would not let herself be seen before any one, and shut herself up in her chamber, and the maiden Maleen had to bring her food from the kitchen.

2.6 Als der Tag herankam, wo die Braut mit dem
Bräutigam in die Kirche gehen sollte, so schämte
sie sich ihrer Häßlichkeit und fürchtete, wenn sie
sich auf der Straße zeigte, würde sie von den Leuten
verspottet und ausgelacht.

When the day approached when the bride was to go to
church with the bridegroom, she was ashamed of her
ugliness and feared that if she showed herself in the street,
people would mock and laugh at her.

2.7 Da sprach sie zur Jungfrau Maleen,

So she said to the maiden Maleen,

2.8 »Dir steht ein großes Glück bevor,

"You are in for a great fortune,

2.9 ich habe mir den Fuß vertreten und kann nicht gut
über die Straße gehen;

I have hurt my foot and cannot walk well in the street;

2.10 du sollst meine Brautkleider anziehen und meine
Stelle einnehmen:

you shall put on my wedding garments and take my place:

2.11 eine größere Ehre kann dir nicht zu teil werden.«

no greater honor can be bestowed on you."

2.12 Die Jungfrau Maleen aber schlug es aus und sagte,

But the maiden refused, saying,

2.13 »Ich verlange keine Ehre, die mir nicht gebührt.«

"I ask no honor that is not due me."

2.14 Es war auch vergeblich, daß sie ihr Gold anbot.

It was also in vain that she offered her gold.

Endlich spracht sie zornig: »Wenn du mir nicht gehorchst,   2.15
At last she said angrily, "If you do not obey me,

so kostet es dir dein Leben: ich brauche nur ein Wort zu sagen,   2.16
it will cost you your life: I need only say the word,

so wird dir der Kopf vor die Füße gelegt.«   2.17
and your head will be laid at your feet."

Da mußte sie gehorchen und die prächtigen Kleider der Braut samt ihrem Schmuck anlegen.   2.18
So she had to obey and put on the bride's splendid clothes and jewelry.

Als sie in den königlichen Saal eintrat, erstaunten alle über ihre große Schönheit, und der König sagte zu seinem Sohne: 2.19
When she entered the royal hall, everyone was amazed at her great beauty, and the king said to his son,

»Das ist die Braut, die ich dir ausgewählt habe und die du zur Kirche führen sollst.«   2.20
"This is the bride I have chosen for you and whom you are to lead to the church."

Der Bräutigam erstaunte und dachte: 2.21
The bridegroom was astonished and thought:

»Sie gleicht meiner Jungfrau Maleen, und ich würde glauben, sie wäre es selbst aber die sitzt schon lange im Turm gefangen oder ist tot.«   2.22
"She resembles my maiden, Maleen, and I would believe it to be her, but she has long been imprisoned in the tower or is dead."

2.23 **Er nahm sie an der Hand und führte sie zur Kirche.**
He took her by the hand and led her to the church.

2.24 **An dem Wege stand ein Brennesselbusch, da sprach sie:**
There was a stinging nettle bush by the road, and she spoke:

»Brennettelbusch,	"Brennettelbusch,
Brennettelbusch so klene,	Brennettelbusch so klene,
wat steist du hier allene?	What are you doing here?
Ik hef de Tyt geweten,	I hef de Tyt geweten,
da hef ik dy ungesaden,	I didn't like that,
ungebraden eten.«	unused. "

4.1 **»Was sprichst du da?« fragte der Königssohn.**
"What are you talking about?" asked the king's son.

4.2 **»Nichts.« antwortete sie,**
"Nothing." she replied,

4.3 **»ich dachte nur an die Jungfrau Maleen.«**
"I was only thinking of the maiden Maleen."

4.4 **Er verwunderte sich, daß sie von ihr wußte, schwieg aber still.**
He was surprised that she knew about her, but remained silent.

271

Als sie an den Steg vor dem Kirchhof kamen,   4.5
When they came to the footbridge in front of the
churchyard,

sprach sie: 4.6
she spoke:

»Karkstegels, brik nich,   "Karkstegels, brik nich,

bün de rechte Brut nich.«   bün de rechte Brut nich."

»Was sprichst du da?« fragte der Königssohn.   6.1
"What are you talking about?" asked the king's son.

»Nichts.« antwortete sie,   6.2
"Nothing." she replied,

»ich dachte nur an die Jungfrau Maleen.«   6.3
"I was just thinking about the maiden Maleen."

»Kennst du die Jungfrau Maleen?«   6.4
"Do you know the maiden Maleen?"

»Nein.« antwortete sie, »wie sollt ich sie kennen,   6.5
"No." she replied, "how could I know her,

ich habe nur von ihr gehört.« Als sie an die Kirchthür   6.6
kamen,
I've only heard of her." When they came to the church
door,

sprach sie abermals: 6.7
she spoke again:

»Karkendär, brik nich,   "Karkendär, brik nich,

bün de rechte Brut nich.«   bün de rechte Brut nich."

8.1 »Was sprichst du da.« fragte er. »Ach.« antwortete sie,
"What are you talking about." he asked. "Oh." she replied,

8.2 »ich habe nur an die Jungfrau Maleen gedacht.«
"I was just thinking about the maiden Maleen."

8.3 Da zog er ein kostbares Geschmeide hervor,
Then he pulled out a precious jewel,

8.4 legte es ihr um den Hals und hakte die Kettenringe ineinander.
put it around her neck and hooked the chain rings together.

8.5 Darauf traten sie in die Kirche und der Priester legte vor dem Altar ihre Hände ineinander und vermählte sie.
They then entered the church and the priest placed their hands together in front of the altar and married them.

8.6 Er führte sie zurück,
He led her back,

8.7 aber sie sprach auf dem ganzen Wege kein Wort.
but she did not speak a word the whole way.

Als sie wieder in dem königlichen Schloß angelangt
waren, eilte sie in die Kammer der Braut, legte die
prächtigen Kleider und den Schmuck ab, zog ihren
grauen Kittel an und behielt nur das Geschmeide
um den Hals, das sie von dem Bräutigam empfangen
hatte.   8.8

When they arrived back at the royal palace, she hurried
into the bride's chamber, took off her splendid clothes
and jewels, put on her gray gown, and kept only the
jewels around her neck that she had received from the
bridegroom.

Als die Nacht heran kam und die Braut in das Zimmer
des Königssohns sollte geführt werden, so ließ sie den
Schleier über ihr Gesicht fallen, damit er den Betrug
nicht merken sollte.   8.9

When night came on and the bride was to be led into the
king's son's room, she let the veil fall over her face so that
he would not notice the deception.

Sobald alle Leute fortgegangen waren, sprach er zu
ihr: 8.10

As soon as all the people had gone away, he said to her,

»Was hast du doch zu dem Brennesselbusch gesagt,
der an dem Wege stand?«   8.11

"What did you say to the nettle-bush that stood by the
road?"

»Zu welchem Brennesselbusch?« fragte sie,   8.12

"To which nettle-bush?" she asked,

»ich spreche mit keinem Brennesselbusch.«   8.13

"I am not talking to any nettle- bush."

»Wenn du es nicht gethan hast,   8.14

"If you have not done so,

8.15 so bist du die rechte Braut nicht.« sagte er.
you are not the right bride. " said he.

8.16 Da half sie sich und sprach:
Then she helped herself and spoke:

»Mut heruet na myne Maegt,	"Mut heruet na myne Maegt,
de my myn Gedanken draegt.«	de my myn thoughts draegt."

10.1 Sie ging hinaus und fuhr die Jungfrau Maleen an: »Dirne,
She went out and said to the maiden Maleen: "Maiden,

10.2 was hast du zu dem Brennesselbusch gesagt?«
what did you say to the nettle bush?"

10.3 »Ich sagte nichts als:
"I said nothing but:

»Brennettelbusch,	"Brennettelbusch,
Brennettelbusch so klene,	Brennettelbusch so klene,
wat steist du hier allene?	What are you doing here?
Ik hef de Tyt geweten,	I hef de Tyt geweten,
da hef ik dy ungesaden,	I didn't like that,
ungebraden eten.«	unused. "

Die Braut lief in die Kammer zurück und sagte,   12.1
The bride ran back into the chamber and said,

»Jetzt weiß ich, was ich zu dem Brennesselbusch   12.2
gesprochen habe.«
"Now I know what I said to the nettle bush."

und wiederholte die Worte, die sie eben gehört hatte.   12.3
and repeated the words she had just heard.

»Aber was sagtest du zu dem Kirchensteg, als wir   12.4
darüber gingen?«
"But what did you say to the church footbridge when we
were walking over it?"

fragte der Königssohn. »Zu dem Kirchensteg?«   12.5
asked the king's son. "To the footbridge?"

antwortete sie, »ich spreche mit keinem   12.6
Kirchensteg.«
she replied, "I do not speak to any footbridge."

»Dann bist du auch die rechte Braut nicht.« Sie sagte   12.7
wiederum:
"Then you are not the right bride either." She said again:

»Mut heruet na myne   "Mut heruet na myne
Maegt,   Maegt,

de my myn Gedanken   de my myn thoughts
draegt.«   draegt."

Lief hinaus und fuhr die Jungfrau Maleen an: »Dirne,   14.1
Ran out and said to the maiden Maleen: "Maiden,

was hast du zu dem Kirchsteg gesagt?«   14.2
what did you say to the footbridge?"

14.3 »Ich sagte nichts als:
"I said nothing but:

»Karkstegels, brik nich,   "Karkstegels, brik nich,

bün de rechte Brut nich.«   bün de rechte Brut nich."

16.1 »Das kostet dich dein Leben.«
"That will cost you your life."

16.2 rief die Braut, eilte aber in die Kammer und sagte,
cried the bride, but she hurried into the chamber and said,

16.3 »Jetzt weiß ich, was ich zu dem Kirchsteg gesprochen habe.«,
"Now I know what I said to the church door.",

16.4 und wiederholte die Worte.
and repeated the words.

16.5 »Aber was sagtest du zur Kirchenthür?«
"But what did you say to the church door?"

16.6 »Zur Kirchenthür?« antwortete sie,
"To the church door?" she answered,

16.7 »ich spreche mit keiner Kirchenthür.«
"I do not speak to any church door."

16.8 »Dann bist du auch die rechte Braut nicht.«
"Then you are not the right bride."

16.9 Sie ging hinaus, fuhr die Jungfrau Maleen an: »Dirne,
She went out and said to the maiden: "Maiden,

was hast du zu der Kirchenthür gesagt?«   16.10
what did you say to the church door?"

»Ich sagte nichts als: 16.11
"I said nothing but:

»Karkendär, brik nich,   "Karkendär, brik nich,

bün de rechte Brut nich.«   bün de rechte Brut nich."

»Das bricht dir den Hals.«   18.1
"That will break your neck."

rief die Braut und geriet in den größten Zorn, eilte   18.2
aber zurück in die Kammer und sagte,
cried the bride, in a great rage, but she hurried back into
the chamber and said,

»Jetzt weiß ich, was ich zu der Kirchenthür   18.3
gesprochen habe.«
"Now I know what I said at the church door."

und wiederholte die Worte.   18.4
and repeated the words.

»Aber wo hast du das Geschmeide, das ich dir an der   18.5
Kirchenthür gab?«
"But where have you the jewels I gave you at the church
door?"

»Was für ein Geschmeide?« antwortete sie,   18.6
"What jewels?" she answered,

»du hast mir kein Geschmeide gegeben.«   18.7
"you gave me no jewels."

18.8 »Ich habe es dir selbst um den Hals gelegt und selbst eingehakt;
"I put it around your neck myself and hooked it on myself;

18.9 wenn du das nicht weißt, so bist du die rechte Braut nicht.«
if you don't know that, then you are not the right bride."

18.10 Er zog ihr den Schleier vom Gesicht, und als er ihre grundlose Häßlichkeit erblickte, sprang er erschrocken zurück und sprach,
He pulled the veil from her face, and when he saw her gratuitous ugliness, he jumped back in horror and said,

18.11 »Wie kommst du hierher? wer bist du?«
"How came you here? who are you?"

18.12 »Ich bin deine verlobte Braut, aber weil ich fürchtete, die Leute würden mich verspotten, wenn sie mich draußen erblickten, so habe ich dem Aschenputtel befohlen, meine Kleider anzuziehen und statt meiner zur Kirche zu gehen.«
"I am your betrothed bride, but because I was afraid that people would mock me if they saw me outside, I ordered Cinderella to put on my clothes and go to church instead of me."

18.13 »Wo ist das Mädchen?« sagte er, »ich will es sehen,
"Where is the girl?" he said, "I want to see her,

18.14 geh und hol es hierher.«
go and fetch her here."

Sie ging hinaus und sagte den Dienern, das
Aschenputtel sei eine Betrügerin, sie sollten es in
den Hof hinabführen und ihm den Kopf abschlagen.
18.15

She went out and told the servants that Cinderella was
an impostor and that they should take her down to the
courtyard and cut off her head.

Die Diener packten es und wollten es fortschleppen,
aber es schrie so laut um Hilfe, daß der Königssohn
seine Stimme vernahm, aus seinem Zimmer
herbeieilte und den Befehl gab, das Mädchen
augenblicklich loszulassen.
18.16

The servants seized her and wanted to drag her away, but
she cried so loudly for help that the king's son heard her
voice, rushed out of his room and gave orders to let the girl
go at once.

Es wurden Lichter herbeigeholt, und da bemerkte er
an ihrem Hals den Goldschmuck, den er ihm vor der
Kirchenthür gegeben hatte.
18.17

Lights were brought in, and then he noticed on her neck
the gold jewelry he had given her at the church door.

»Du bist die rechte Braut.« sagte er,
18.18

"You are the right bride." he said,

»die mit mir zur Kirche gegangen ist:
18.19

"who has gone to church with me:

komm mit mir in meine Kammer.«
18.20

come with me to my chamber."

Als sie beide allein waren, sprach er,
18.21

When they were both alone, he said,

18.22 »Du hast auf dem Kirchgang die Jungfrau Maleen genannt,

"You called the maiden Maleen at church,

18.23 die meine verlobte Braut war.

who was my betrothed bride.

18.24 Wenn ich dächte, es wäre möglich, so müßte ich glauben, sie stände vor mir, du gleichst ihr in allem.«

If I thought it were possible, I should believe that she stood before me, that you were like her in everything."

18.25 Sie antwortete:

She replied:

18.26 »Ich bin die Jungfrau Maleen, die um dich sieben Jahre in der Finsternis gefangen gesessen, Hunger und Durst gelitten und so lange in Not und Armut gelebt hat.

"I am the maiden Maleen, who was imprisoned in darkness for you for seven years, suffered hunger and thirst and lived so long in need and poverty.

18.27 Aber heute bescheint mich die Sonne wieder.

But today the sun is shining on me again.

18.28 Ich bin dir in der Kirche angetraut und bin deine rechtmäßige Gemahlin.«

I am married to you in the church and am your lawful wife."

18.29 Da küßten sie einander und waren glücklich für ihr Lebtag.

Then they kissed each other and were happy for the rest of their lives.

Der falschen Braut ward zur Vergeltung der Kopf abgeschlagen. 18.30
The false bride's head was cut off in retribution.

Der Turm, in welchem die Jungfrau Maleen gesessen 19.1
hatte, stand noch lange Zeit, und wenn die Kinder
vorüber gingen, so sangen sie:
The tower in which the maiden Maleen had sat stood for a
long time, and when the children passed by, they sang:

»Kling, klang, kloria,   "Clink, clink, clink,

wer sitt in dissen Thoria?   Who sits in dissen Thoria?

Dar sitt en   Dar sitt en
Königsdochter in,   Königsdochter in,

die kann ik nich to seen   I can't see them.
krygn.

De Muer de will nich   De Muer de will nicht
bräken,   bräken,

de Steen de will nich   de Steen de will nich
stechen.   sting.

Hänschen mit de bunte Jak,   Hänschen with the colorful Jak,

kumm unn folg my   come and follow me
achterna.«   back."

Der Stiefel von Büffelleder

The Boot of Buffalo Leather

1.1 Ein Soldat, der sich vor nichts fürchtet, kümmert sich auch um nichts.

A soldier who fears nothing cares for nothing.

1.2 So einer hatte seinen Abschied erhalten, und da er nichts gelernt hatte und nichts verdienen konnte, so zog er umher und bat gute Leute um ein Almosen.

Such a man had received his discharge, and as he had learned nothing and could earn nothing, he went about asking good people for alms.

1.3 Auf seinen Schultern hing ein alter Wettermantel,

An old weather coat hung on his shoulders,

1.4 und ein Paar Reiterstiefel von Büffelleder waren ihm auch noch geblieben.

and he still had a pair of buffalo-leather riding boots.

1.5 Eines Tages ging er, ohne auf Weg und Steg zu achten, immer ins Feld hinein und gelangte endlich in einen Wald.

One day, without paying attention to the path or the footbridge, he kept walking into the field and finally came to a forest.

Er wußte nicht wo er war, sah aber auf einem abgehauenen Baumstamm einen Mann sitzen, der gut gekleidet war und einen grünen Jägerrock trug. 1.6
He didn't know where he was, but saw a well-dressed man wearing a green hunter's coat sitting on a cut-down tree trunk.

Der Soldat reichte ihm die Hand, 1.7
The soldier reached out his hand,

ließ sich neben ihm auf das Gras nieder und streckte seine Beine aus. 1.8
sat down on the grass next to him and stretched out his legs.

»Ich sehe, du hast feine Stiefel an, die glänzend gewichst sind.« 1.9
"I see you're wearing fine boots with a shiny wadding."

sagte er zu dem Jäger, 1.10
he said to the hunter,

»wenn du aber herumziehen müßtest wie ich, 1.11
"but if you had to move around like me,

so würden sie nicht lange halten. 1.12
they wouldn't last long.

Schau die meinigen an, die sind von Büffelleder und haben schon lange gedient gehen aber durch dick und dünn.« 1.13
Look at mine, they are made of buffalo leather and have served for a long time, but they go through thick and thin."

Nach einer Weile stand der Soldat auf und sprach: 1.14
After a while, the soldier stood up and said:

1.15 »Ich kann nicht länger bleiben, der Hunger treibt mich fort.
"I can't stay any longer, hunger is driving me away.

1.16 Aber, Bruder Wichsstiefel, wohinaus geht der Weg?«
But, brother wanker, where are you going?"

1.17 »Ich weiß es selber nicht.« antwortete der Jäger,
"I don't know myself." replied the hunter,

1.18 »ich habe mich in dem Walde verirrt.«
"I've lost my way in the forest."

1.19 »So geht dir's ja wie mir.« sprach der Soldat,
"You're like me." said the soldier,

1.20 »gleich und gleich gesellt sich gern,
"birds of a feather flock together,

1.21 wir wollen bei einander bleiben und den Weg suchen.«
let's stay together and look for the way."

1.22 Der Jäger lächelte ein wenig und sie gingen zusammen fort immer weiter, bis die Nacht einbrach.
The hunter smiled a little and they walked on together until night fell.

1.23 »Wir kommen aus dem Walde nicht heraus.« sprach der Soldat,
"We can't get out of the forest." said the soldier,

1.24 »aber ich sehe dort in der Ferne ein Licht schimmern,
"but I can see a light shimmering in the distance,

da wird's etwas zu essen geben.« Sie fanden ein Steinhaus, 1.25

there will be something to eat." They found a stone house,

klopften an die Thür und ein altes Weib öffnete. 1.26

knocked on the door and an old woman opened it.

»Wir suchen ein Nachtquartier.« 1.27

"We're looking for a place to stay for the night."

sprach her Soldat, »und etwas Unterfutter für den Magen, 1.28

said the soldier, "and some food for our stomachs,

denn der meinige ist so leer wie ein alter Tornister.« 1.29

because mine is as empty as an old knapsack."

»Hier könnt ihr nicht bleiben.« 1.30

"You cannot stay here."

antwortete die Alte, »das ist ein Räuberhaus, und ihr thut am klügsten, daß ihr euch fortmacht, bevor sie heim kommen, denn finden sie euch, so seid ihr verloren.« 1.31

replied the old woman, "this is a robbers' house, and you had best get away before they come home, for if they find you, you will be lost."

»Es wird so schlimm nicht sein.« antwortete der Soldat, 1.32

"It will not be so bad." replied the soldier,

»ich habe seit zwei Tagen keinen Bissen genossen, und es ist mir einerlei, ob ich hier umkomme oder im Walde vor Hunger sterbe. 1.33

"I have not had a morsel for two days, and it is all the same to me whether I perish here or die of hunger in the forest.

1.34 Ich gehe herein.« Der Jäger wollte nicht folgen,
I am going in." The hunter didn't want to follow,

1.35 aber der Soldat zog ihn am Ärmel mit sich:
but the soldier pulled him along by the sleeve:

1.36 »Komm, Bruderherz, es wird nicht gleich an den Kragen gehen.«
"Come on, brother, it won't go straight to the collar."

1.37 Die Alte hatte Mitleid und sagte,
The old woman took pity on him and said,

1.38 »Kriecht hinter den Ofen;
"Crawl behind the stove;

1.39 wenn sie etwas übrig lassen und eingeschlafen sind,
if they leave anything and fall asleep,

1.40 so will ich's euch zustecken.«
I'll slip it to you."

1.41 Kaum saßen sie in der Ecke, so kamen zwölf Räuber herein gestürmt, setzten sich an den Tisch, der schon gedeckt war und forderten mit Ungestüm das Essen.
As soon as they were sitting in the corner, twelve robbers came rushing in, sat down at the table, which was already laid, and demanded food with impetuosity.

1.42 Die Alte trug einen großen Braten herein,
The old woman brought in a large roast,

1.43 und die Räuber ließen sich's wohl schmecken.
and the robbers enjoyed it.

Als der Geruch von der Speise dem Soldaten in die
Nase stieg,   1.44
When the smell of the food caught the soldier's nose,

sagte er zum Jäger: »Ich halt's nicht länger aus,   1.45
he said to the hunter: "I can't stand it any longer,

ich setze mich an den Tisch und esse mit.«   1.46
I'll sit down at the table and eat with you."

»Du bringst uns ums Leben.«   1.47
"You're killing us."

sprach der Jäger und hielt ihn am Arm.   1.48
said the hunter, holding him by the arm.

Aber der Soldat fing an laut zu husten.   1.49
But the soldier began to cough loudly.

Als die Räuber das hörten, warfen sie Messer und   1.50
Gabel hin, sprangen auf und entdeckten die beiden
hinter dem Ofen.
When the robbers heard this, they threw down their knives
and forks, jumped up and discovered the two of them
behind the stove.

»Aha, ihr Herren.« riefen sie,   1.51
"Aha, you gentlemen." they shouted,

»sitzt ihr in der Ecke? Was wollt ihr hier?   1.52
"are you sitting in the corner? What are you doing here?

Seid ihr als Kundschafter ausgeschickt? Wartet,   1.53
Have you been sent out as scouts? Wait,

ihr sollt an einem dürren Ast das Fliegen lernen.«   1.54
you're supposed to learn to fly on a dry branch."

288

1.55 »Nur manierlich.« sprach der Soldat,
"Only mannerly." said the soldier,

1.56 »mich hungert, gebt mir zu essen, hernach könnt ihr mit mir machen was ihr wollt.«
"I'm hungry, give me something to eat, then you can do what you like with me."

1.57 Die Räuber stutzten und der Anführer sprach:
The robbers were astonished and the leader said,

1.58 »Ich sehe, du fürchtest dich nicht, gut, Essen sollst du haben, aber hernach mußt du sterben.«
"I see you are not afraid, fine, you shall have food, but afterwards you must die."

1.59 »Das wird sich finden.« sagte der Soldat,
"I'll see to that." said the soldier,

1.60 setzte sich an den Tisch und fing an tapfer in den Braten einzuhauen.
sat down at the table and began to bravely dig into the roast.

1.61 »Bruder Wichsstiefel, komm und iß.« rief er dem Jäger zu,
"Brother wanker, come and eat." he called to the hunter,

1.62 »du wirst hungrig sein, so gut als ich, und einen besseren Braten kannst du zu Hause nicht haben!«
"you'll be hungry, as good as I am, and you can't have a better roast at home!"

1.63 aber der Jäger wollte nicht essen.
but the hunter refused to eat.

Die Räuber sahen dem Soldaten mit Erstaunen zu und sagten, 1.64
The robbers watched the soldier in astonishment and said,

»Der Kerl macht keine Umstände.« Hernach sprach er, 1.65
"The fellow's no trouble." Then he said,

»Das Essen wäre schon gut, 1.66
"The food would be fine,

nun schafft auch einen guten Trunk herbei.« 1.67
now bring a good drink."

Der Anführer war in der Laune, sich das auch noch gefallen zu lassen und rief der Alten zu: 1.68
The leader was in a mood to put up with this and called out to the old woman:

»Hol eine Flasche aus dem Keller und zwar von dem besten.« 1.69
"Get a bottle from the cellar, the best one."

Der Soldat zog den Pfropfen heraus, daß es knallte, ging mit der Flasche zu dem Jäger und sprach: 1.70
The soldier pulled out the stopper so that it cracked, went to the huntsman with the bottle and said:

»Gieb acht, Bruder, du sollst dein blaues Wunder sehen: 1.71
"Take care, brother, you shall see your blue miracle:

jetzt will ich eine Gesundheit auf die ganze Sippschaft ausbringen.« 1.72
now I want to bring health to the whole clan."

290

1.73   Dann schwenkte er die Flasche über den Köpfen der Räuber, rief,

Then he waved the bottle over the heads of the robbers, cried,

1.74   »Ihr sollt alle leben,

"You shall all live,

1.75   aber das Maul auf und die rechte Hand in der Höhe.«

but keep your mouths open and your right hands up."

1.76   und that einen herzhaften Zug.

and took a hearty draught.

1.77   Kaum waren die Worte heraus, so saßen sie alle bewegungslos als wären sie von Stein, hatten das Maul offen und streckten den rechten Arm in die Höhe.

As soon as the words were out, they all sat motionless as if they were made of stone, with their mouths open and their right arms stretched upwards.

1.78   Der Jäger sprach zu dem Soldaten:

The hunter said to the soldier,

1.79   »Ich sehe, du kannst noch andere Kunststücke, aber nun komm und laß uns heimgehen.«

"I see you can do other tricks, but now come and let us go home."

1.80   »Oho, Bruderherz, das wäre zu früh abmarschiert, wir haben den Feind geschlagen und wollen erst Beute machen.

"Oho, brother, that would be too early to march off, we have beaten the enemy and want to get some booty first.

Die sitzen da fest und sperren das Maul vor   1.81
Verwunderung auf: sie dürfen sich aber nicht rühren,
bis ich es erlaube.
They are sitting there, their mouths open in astonishment,
but they must not move until I give them permission.

Komm, iß und trink.«   1.82
Come, eat and drink."

Die Alte mußte noch eine Flasche von dem besten   1.83
holen, und der Soldat stand nicht eher auf, als bis er
wieder für drei Tage gegessen hatte.
The old woman had to fetch another bottle of the best, and
the soldier did not get up till he had eaten again for three
days.

Endlich als der Tag kam, sagte er: 1.84
At last, when day came, he said,

»Nun ist es Zeit, daß wir das Zelt abbrechen, und   1.85
damit wir einen kurzen Marsch haben, so soll die
Alte uns den nächsten Weg nach der Stadt zeigen.«
"Now it is time for us to break down the tent, and that we
may have a short march, let the old woman show us the
nearest way to the town."

Als sie dort angelangt waren, ging er zu seinen alten   1.86
Kameraden und sprach:
When they had arrived there, he went to his old comrades
and said,

»Ich habe draußen im Walde ein Nest voll   1.87
Galgenvögel aufgefunden, kommt mit, wir wollen
es ausheben.«
"I have found a nest full of gallows-birds out in the forest;
come along, let us dig it out."

1.88 Der Soldat führte sie an und sprach zu dem Jäger:
The soldier led them and said to the hunter:

1.89 »Du mußt wieder mit zurück und zusehen wie sie flattern, wenn wir sie an den Füßen packen.«
"You must go back with us and watch how they flutter when we grab them by the feet."

1.90 Er stellte die Mannschaft rings um die Räuber herum, dann nahm er die Flasche, trank einen Schluck, schwenkte sie über ihnen her und rief:
He placed the crew around the robbers, then took the bottle, drank a sip, waved it over them and shouted:

1.91 »Ihr sollt alle leben!«
"You shall all live!"

1.92 Augenblicklich hatten sie ihre Bewegung wieder,
They immediately regained their movement,

1.93 wurden aber niedergeworfen und an Händen und Füßen mit Stricken gebunden.
but were thrown down and bound hand and foot with ropes.

1.94 Dann hieß sie der Soldat wie Säcke auf einen Wagen werfen und sagte:
Then the soldier ordered them to be thrown like sacks onto a cart and said:

1.95 »Fahrt sie nur gleich vor das Gefängnis.«
"Drive them straight to the prison."

1.96 Der Jäger aber nahm einen von der Mannschaft beiseite und gab ihm noch eine Bestellung mit.
But the huntsman took one of the crew aside and gave him another order.

»Bruder Wichsstiefel.« sprach der Soldat,   2.1
"Brother wankboots." said the soldier,

»wir haben den Feind glücklich überrumpelt und uns   2.2
wohlgenährt,
"we have happily taken the enemy by surprise and fed
ourselves well,

jetzt wollen wir als Nachzügler in aller Ruhe   2.3
hinterher marschieren.«
now we want to march after them in peace and quiet."

Als sie sich der Stadt näherten, so sah der Soldat,   2.4
wie sich eine Menge Menschen aus dem Stadtthor
drängten, lautes Freudengeschrei erhoben und grüne
Zweige in der Lust schwangen.
As they approached the town, the soldier saw a crowd of
people crowding out of the town gate, shouting loudly and
waving green branches in joy.

Dann sah er, daß die ganze Leibwache herangezogen   2.5
kam.
Then he saw that the whole bodyguard had come out.

»Was soll das heißen?« sprach er ganz verwundert zu   2.6
dem Jäger.
"What do you mean?" he said to the huntsman in
astonishment.

»Weißt du nicht.« antwortete er,   2.7
"Don't you know." he replied,

»daß der König lange Zeit aus seinem Reiche entfernt   2.8
war, heute kehrt er zurück, und da gehen ihm alle
entgegen.«
"that the king has been away from his kingdom for a long
time, and today he is returning, and everyone is going to
meet him."

2.9 »Aber wo ist der König.« sprach der Soldat,
"But where is the king." said the soldier,

2.10 »ich sehe ihn nicht.«
"I do not see him."

2.11 »Hier ist er.« antwortete der Jäger,
"Here he is." replied the huntsman,

2.12 »ich bin der König und habe meine Ankunft melden lassen.«
"I am the king, and I have sent word of my arrival."

2.13 Dann öffnete er seinen Jägerrock, daß man die königlichen Kleider sehen konnte.
Then he opened his huntsman's coat so that the king's clothes could be seen.

2.14 Der Soldat erschrak, fiel auf die Knie und bat ihn um Vergebung, daß er ihn in der Unwissenheit wie seinesgleichen behandelt und ihn mit solchem Namen angeredet habe.
The soldier was startled, fell on his knees, and begged his forgiveness for having treated him in ignorance as his equal, and for having called him by such a name.

2.15 Der König aber reichte ihm die Hand und sprach,
But the king shook his hand and said,

2.16 »Du bist ein braver Soldat und hast mir das Leben gerettet.
"You are a good soldier and have saved my life.

2.17 Du sollst keine Not mehr leiden,
You shall suffer no more hardship,

2.18 ich will schon für dich sorgen.
I will take care of you.

Und wenn du einmal ein Stück guten Braten essen 2.19
willst, so gut als in dem Räuberhause, so komm nur
in die königliche Küche.
And if you ever want to eat a piece of good roast meat,
as good as in the robbers' house, just come to the royal
kitchen.

Willst du aber eine Gesundheit ausbringen, 2.20
But if you want to eat something healthy,

so sollst du erst bei mir Erlaubnis dazu holen.« 2.21
you must first get permission from me."

Möwenstein Books

www.mowenstein.com

Renowned Authors

H. G. Wells · Ernest Hemingway
H. P. Lovecraft · Lewis Carroll
Franz Kafka · Friedrich Nietzsche
Albert Einstein · Oscar Wilde
Hans Christian Andersen

Notable Works

Frankenstein · *Alice in Wonderland*
Heart of Darkness · *The Great Gatsby*
Siddhartha · *The Metamorphosis*
Thus Spoke Zarathustra

Translation Services

We offer translation services in various languages, including German, Spanish, Chinese, Korean, Arabic, and more. For custom translations or revisions, please contact us at:

Email: translation@mowenstein.com

Our Collections

Franz Kafka Collection

- The Metamorphosis / Die Verwandlung
- The Trial / Der Prozess
- The Castle / Das Schloss
- and many more...

Pakt mit dem Teufel

- Faust Parts I & II by Johann Wolfgang von Goethe
- Doctor Faustus by Christopher Marlowe

Portraits of Irishmen

- The Picture of Dorian Gray by Oscar Wilde
- A Portrait of the Artist as a Young Man by James Joyce

Children's Classics

- Winnie-the-Pooh / Pu der Bär
- Brothers Grimm Fairy Tales
- Fairy Tales Told for Children
    - Author: Hans Christian Andersen

Visit Us

At Möwenstein Books, we are committed to providing high-quality bilingual editions of classic works. Explore our collections and discover more titles across various genres and languages.

Website: www.mowenstein.com